REVISE EDEXCEL GCSE
ICT

REVISION GUIDE

Series Consultant: Harry Smith   Authors: Nicola Hughes and David Waller

THE REVISE EDEXCEL SERIES
Available in print or online

Online editions for all titles in the Revise Edexcel series are available Autumn 2012.

Presented on our ActiveLearn platform, you can view the full book and customise it by adding notes, comments and weblinks.

Print editions

ICT Revision Guide	9781446903872
ICT Revision Workbook	9781446903896

Online editions

ICT Revision Guide	9781446903834
ICT Revision Workbook	9781446903841

This Revision Guide is designed to complement your classroom and home learning, and to help prepare you for the exam. It does not include all the content and skills needed for the complete course. It is designed to work in combination with Edexcel's main GCSE ICT 2010 series.

To find out more visit
www.pea ... xcelgcseICTrevision

ALWAYS LEARNING   PEARSON

Contents

PERSONAL DIGITAL DEVICES

1   Uses of digital devices
2   Using digital devices
3   Common features
4   Input and output devices
5   Connectivity
6   Mobile phones 1
7   Mobile phones 2
8   Personal computers 1
9   Personal computers 2
10 Cameras and camcorders 1
11 Cameras and camcorders 2
12 Media players 1
13 Media players 2
14 Games consoles 1
15 Games consoles 2
16 Home entertainment systems
17 Satellite navigation 1
18 Satellite navigation 2
19 Impact on organisations

CONNECTIVITY

20 Home networks
21 Network security
22 Combining technologies
23 Bandwidth and latency
24 Wi-Fi and mobile broadband
25 Peer-to-peer networks
26 Communication protocols 1
27 Communication protocols 2
28 Security risks in a network
29 Physical security risks

OPERATING ONLINE

30 The Internet
31 Internet use 1
32 Internet use 2
33 Security measures
34 Personal spaces
35 Information misuse
36 Preventing misuse
37 Legislation
38 Copyright

ONLINE GOODS AND SERVICES

39 Online shopping 1
40 Online shopping 2
41 Online auctions
42 Online education, news and banking
43 Online gaming and entertainment
44 How and why organisations operate online
45 Transactional data
46 Internet advertising 1
47 Internet advertising 2
48 Internet advertising 3
49 Payment systems 1
50 Payment systems 2
51 Consumer protection
52 Applications software
53 Commercial response to SaaS
54 Storage: local or online?
55 Search engines

ONLINE COMMUNITIES

56 Online communities – what are they?
57 Online workspaces and VLEs
58 Social networks
59 User-generated reference sites
60 Social bookmarking sites
61 Creation of knowledge
62 Impact on working practices
63 Socialising and responsible use
64 A global scale

ISSUES

65 Security issues
66 Privacy issues
67 Monitoring movements and communications
68 Health and safety
69 The impact of networks
70 Legislation relating to the use of ICT
71 Unequal access to ICT
72 Safe and responsible practice
73 Sustainability issues

EXAM SKILLS

74 Scenario
75 Command words
76 Reading the question
77 Explaining with examples and reasons
78 Avoiding common mistakes
79 Extended questions

80 Question practice
86 Glossary
90 Answers
106 Space for your own notes

A small bit of small print

Target grade ranges are quoted in this book for some of the questions. Students targeting this grade range should be aiming to get most of the marks available. Students targeting a higher grade should be aiming to get all of the marks available.

Edexcel publishes Sample Assessment Material, the Specification and Technology Update on its website. This is the official content and this book should be used in conjunction with it. The questions in *Now try this* have been written to help you practise every topic in the book. Remember: the real exam questions may not look like this.

See www.pearsonschools.co.uk/edexcelgcseictrevision for the latest updates.

Uses of digital devices

People use digital devices in every aspect of their daily lives. You need to be able to explain how the use of personal digital devices affects everyday life.

Digital devices allow people to **communicate** at any time and wherever they are through:

- text messages (Short Message Service, SMS)
- social networking sites
- instant messaging
- media messages (Multimedia Messaging Service, MMS)
- voice calls
- video calls
- emails.

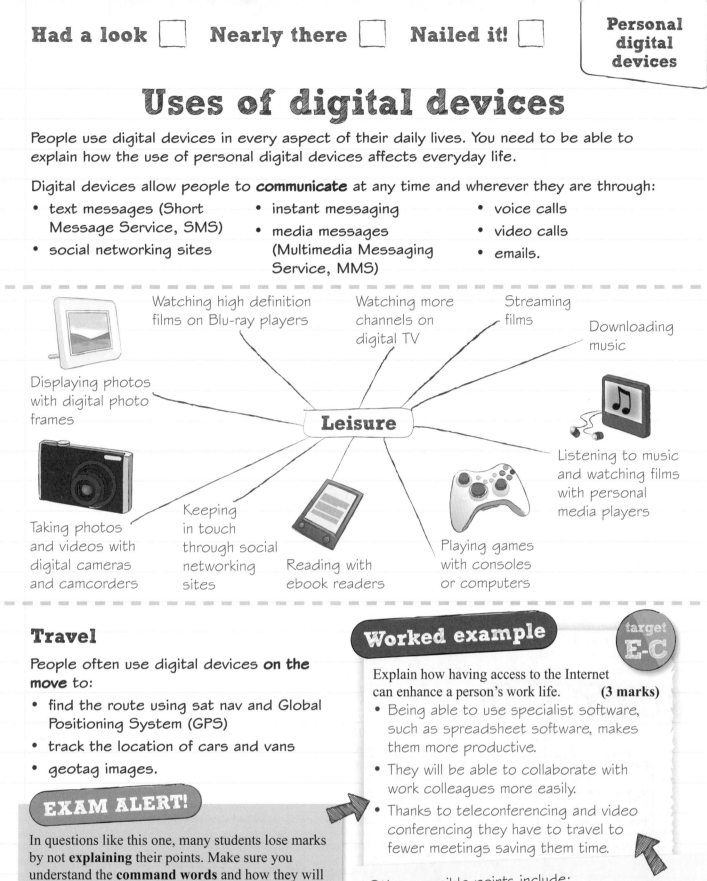

Watching high definition films on Blu-ray players

Watching more channels on digital TV

Streaming films

Downloading music

Displaying photos with digital photo frames

Leisure

Listening to music and watching films with personal media players

Taking photos and videos with digital cameras and camcorders

Keeping in touch through social networking sites

Reading with ebook readers

Playing games with consoles or computers

Travel

People often use digital devices **on the move** to:

- find the route using sat nav and Global Positioning System (GPS)
- track the location of cars and vans
- geotag images.

EXAM ALERT!

In questions like this one, many students lose marks by not **explaining** their points. Make sure you understand the **command words** and how they will be used in your exam paper. When asked to explain you need to make a point with an explanation.

Students have struggled with exam questions similar to this – **be prepared!**

ResultsPlus

Worked example

target
E-C

Explain how having access to the Internet can enhance a person's work life.   **(3 marks)**

- Being able to use specialist software, such as spreadsheet software, makes them more productive.
- They will be able to collaborate with work colleagues more easily.
- Thanks to teleconferencing and video conferencing they have to travel to fewer meetings saving them time.

Other possible points include:
- Improved technology and devices means that it is easier to work from home which saves time.
- They can draw on the expertise of people all around the world.

Now try this

target
F-E

Keziah uses her smartphone to communicate with colleagues at work.
State **two** ways that Keziah might use her smartphone for leisure or travel.   **(2 marks)**

Using digital devices

Digital devices have many **features** and perform many **functions**. You need to understand that different people are looking for different things from their digital devices.

Audience and purpose

When companies design a digital device they have to think about **who** will be using the device (the **audience**) and **how** they will use it (the **purpose**).

Take mobile phones as an example:

- A teenager might want Internet access for accessing social networking sites.
- A business person might want a qwerty keyboard so they can easily send emails.
- An older person might want a large screen and an easy-to-use interface.

Wants versus needs

When choosing a digital device for a particular individual you need to think about **user requirements**. It is important to weigh up what they want against what they need.

Take laptops as an example.

I want...	I need...
as big a widescreen as possible	something small that I can carry easily
a really fast processor	something that is not too expensive

When choosing a device you need to think about a number of important factors.

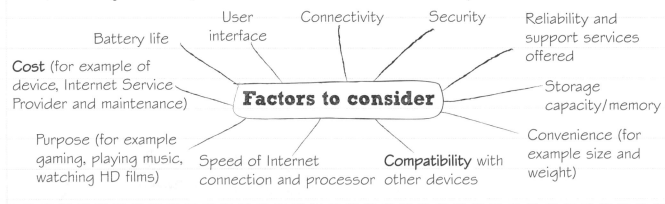

Battery life · User interface · Connectivity · Security · Reliability and support services offered

Cost (for example of device, Internet Service Provider and maintenance)

Factors to consider

Storage capacity/memory

Purpose (for example gaming, playing music, watching HD films) · Speed of Internet connection and processor · **Compatibility** with other devices · Convenience (for example size and weight)

Worked example

	Tablet computer A	Tablet computer B	Tablet computer C
Connectivity	USB 2.0, Wi-Fi	Bluetooth	Wi-Fi
Storage	16 GB	32 GB	8 GB
Processor speed	1.2 GHz	1 GHz	800 MHz
Weight	680 g	220 g	650 g
Size	242 × 190 × 13 mm	150 × 80 × 10 mm	170 × 220 × 14 mm

target **F**

Michael is travelling to an overseas athletics event. He wants to buy a new tablet computer.
Which **one** of these is the most portable?

(1 mark)

☐ Tablet computer A
☒ Tablet computer B
☐ Tablet computer C

Now try this

target **C-A***

*Ryan and Michael take their personal digital devices with them when they travel to international competitions.

Discuss what they need to consider if they want to use their devices when they are away from home.   **(6 marks)**

 The asterisk means that the quality of your written communication will be assessed.

Common features

You need to know about the features that different digital devices have in common.

Processor

There is a **processor** in all digital devices, from desktop computers to mobile phones. It controls all the functions of the device. There are specialist microprocessors for different devices.

Internal memory

While the microprocessor is working it needs to store the program instructions and data in its **internal memory**. Different devices have different amounts of internal memory which is measured in bytes.

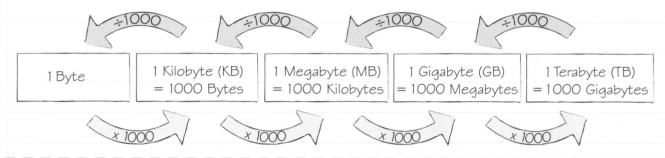

| 1 Byte | 1 Kilobyte (KB) = 1000 Bytes | 1 Megabyte (MB) = 1000 Kilobytes | 1 Gigabyte (GB) = 1000 Megabytes | 1 Terabyte (TB) = 1000 Gigabytes |

Digital devices are storage devices. In addition to their internal memory, digital devices contain components that can store data. For example, computers contain high **capacity** hard disk drives to store terabytes of data. Hard disk drives tend not to be used in portable devices because they contain moving parts and can be easily damaged.

Flash memory

Flash memory is a type of **peripheral** that is ideal for portable digital devices because:

- it **doesn't lose data** when turned off
- it has **no moving parts** so cannot be easily damaged (also known as **solid state**)
- it is removable and can be used to **transfer data** between devices.

Mitch could use a DVD or CD drive to back up his video files.

(a) State **one** reason why DVD is more suitable. **(1 mark)**

DVDs have a larger storage capacity.

(b) Identify **one local** storage device, other than a DVD or CD drive, that could be used for backups. **(1 mark)**

Memory stick.

EXAM ALERT!

Nearly two thirds of students got (a) wrong, thinking that CDs were just for storing music. Almost half of students got (b) wrong. Lots of them didn't notice the word 'local' and incorrectly suggested online storage.

This was a real exam question that a lot of students struggled with – **be prepared!**

ResultsPlus

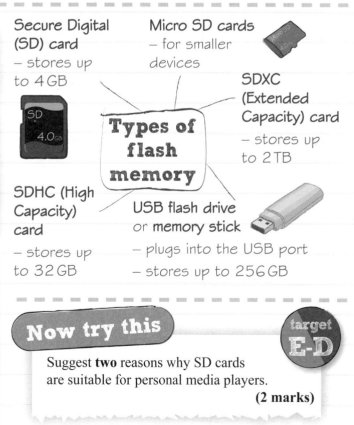

Secure Digital (SD) card
– stores up to 4 GB

Micro SD cards
– for smaller devices

SDXC (Extended Capacity) card
– stores up to 2 TB

Types of flash memory

SDHC (High Capacity) card
– stores up to 32 GB

USB flash drive or **memory stick**
– plugs into the USB port
– stores up to 256 GB

Now try this

target
E-D

Suggest **two** reasons why SD cards are suitable for personal media players.

(2 marks)

Input and output devices

There are three types of **peripherals**: **storage devices**, **input devices** which allow users to give instructions and input data to the device and **output devices** which allow the user to see or hear information after it has been processed.

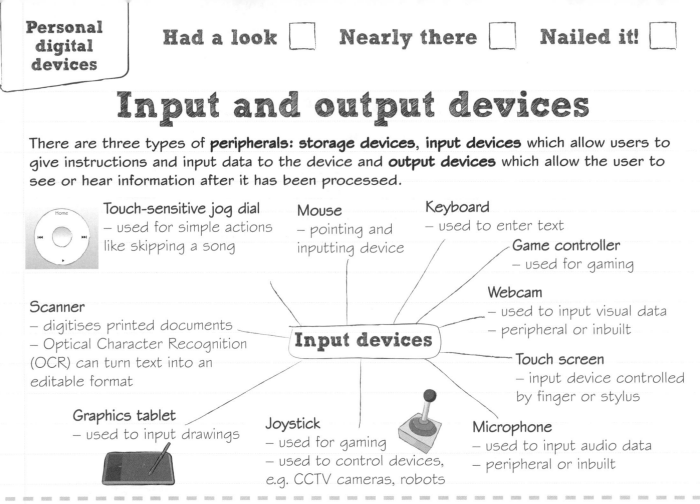

Touch-sensitive jog dial – used for simple actions like skipping a song

Mouse – pointing and inputting device

Keyboard – used to enter text

Game controller – used for gaming

Webcam – used to input visual data – peripheral or inbuilt

Scanner – digitises printed documents – Optical Character Recognition (OCR) can turn text into an editable format

Input devices

Touch screen – input device controlled by finger or stylus

Graphics tablet – used to input drawings

Joystick – used for gaming – used to control devices, e.g. CCTV cameras, robots

Microphone – used to input audio data – peripheral or inbuilt

Output devices

Speakers	– Peripheral or inbuilt device allowing you to hear audio output.
Docking station	– Amplifies audio output of small devices. – Charges device.
Headphones	– Allow just one person to hear audio output.
Printer	– Allows you to produce 'hard copy'.
Headset	– Combines microphone and headphones to input and output audio data.
Screen	– Inbuilt display screens (e.g. laptop, smartphone) or monitor.

Worked example

target **F-E**

Jo has a new games console. State **two** input devices that she might use with it. **(2 marks)**

1 A steering wheel.

2 A balance board.

Other possible answers are:
webcam, microphone, wireless controller and keyboard (for the Internet)

EXAM ALERT!

Make sure you actually include peripherals as your answer. Sometimes students put 'connection leads' as an answer which is incorrect as these are not in themselves peripherals. And make sure you give an **appropriate** peripheral. A mouse is an input device, but it is not suitable for use with a games console.

Students have struggled with exam questions similar to this – **be prepared!** Results Plus

Now try this

target **F-E**

List **two** peripheral devices that could be connected to a personal media player. **(2 marks)**

Connectivity

Digital devices are able to connect to each other and **share data**. You need to understand the types of connection and how devices exchange data.

Data cable connection

The most common method of data cable connection is a **USB** cable. Most mobile phones and media players can connect by USB cable to a computer running the correct **software**.

Bluetooth

- Bluetooth is a technology allowing devices to communicate with each other **wirelessly**. They communicate over **short distances** using radio waves.
- Most modern devices are Bluetooth enabled or a Bluetooth dongle can be attached to a computer as a peripheral.
- Devices can connect to Bluetooth-enabled peripherals such as printers or speakers.

Wi-Fi

- Wi-Fi is another method of **wireless** communication using radio waves.
- Wi-Fi enabled devices can communicate over **longer distances**.
- Most modern devices are Wi-Fi enabled.
- Wi-Fi allows devices to connect with a computer network and the Internet.
- Wi-Fi allows devices to connect to Wi-Fi enabled peripherals such as printers, speakers, scanners and digital projectors.

Synchronising

When two devices, such as a media player and a computer, are connected they can **automatically exchange data**. This is known as **synchronisation**.

Worked example

target C-B

Explain why Simon would want to 'synchronise' his media player. **(3 marks)**

Synchronisation allows two connected devices to swap data automatically. Simon can set the software, for example iTunes, to update his media player with new or changed items on the computer. If he has downloaded a new music file to the computer or changed some contact details, then the software will automatically update the media player. The computer can also update the media player's software if a new update has been downloaded to the computer.

Cloud synchronisation

Now that people have more Wi-Fi enabled devices such as computers, laptops, tablets, smartphones and media players, cloud computing services such as Apple's iCloud, allow them to store all their data files such as music and films, on a **remote server**. They can then access their files from all of their digital devices.

When using iCloud, if you download a song to one of your devices the file is **automatically downloaded to all your devices**. This saves you having to synchronise multiple devices with the computer.

Now try this

target F-E

(a) List **two** methods of wirelessly connecting a media player to a computer. **(2 marks)**

(b) A user is considering buying some wireless external speakers.
Explain why Wi-Fi enabled speakers might be better than Bluetooth. **(2 marks)**

target C-B

Mobile phones 1

The most widely used personal digital device is the mobile phone. You need to understand the features of mobile phones and how they are used differently by different people.

Core functions

- Mobile phones were developed to allow people to make voice calls when they were 'on the move'.
- Later, using the number keys, people were able to send short text messages using SMS.

Added functions

Modern smartphones are **multifunctional devices**. They have gradually taken on functions that were, or are still, done by other devices. Smartphones can perform the functions of personal media players, cameras, laptops, games consoles and sat navs. This is called **convergence**.

Camera/video camera
– take **still images** and capture **video**
– make **video calls**

Internet browsing
– **stream** music and videos

GPS receiver
– pinpoint position on a map
– get local information (e.g. weather)
– use as a **navigational device**

Multifunctional mobile phones

Data storage
– store photos, music and video
– removable storage (e.g. micro SD card) allows easy transfer

Productivity
– learning, financial management, entertainment and travel apps boost productivity and save time

Entertainment
– play music and video
– play games

Now try this

target F-E

(a) Stephen normally uses his mobile phone to make voice calls and send SMSs. He has now purchased a smartphone. List **two** additional ways in which he can use his smartphone to communicate.

(2 marks)

(b) Describe **one** feature of modern mobile phones that has improved the user experience when watching movies.

(2 marks)

target C-B

Mobile phones 2

As well as understanding the features and functions of mobile phones, you also need to know about the wider issues related to owning and using a mobile phone, such as using a phone abroad, ways to keep a phone secure and safe and responsible use.

Worked example

target
B–A

Rosie is choosing a new mobile phone. Some of the phones use different **network bands**.
Describe what is meant by 'network band'.   **(2 marks)**

Mobile phones in different areas of the world use different frequencies or network bands. If users want to use their mobile phones abroad they will have to have a dual band, tri band or, to cover the whole world, a quad band phone.

Using your mobile phone abroad is called **roaming**.

Security

Mobile phones and the data they contain must be kept safe.

👍 **Hide** the phone – over 50% of thefts occur when phones are left in plain sight in cars.

👍 Set a **PIN**, password or biometric lock.

👍 **Lock the SIM card.**

👍 **Record the unique IMEI number** – the mobile service provider can block the phone using this number.

👍 **Restrict Bluetooth usage** – 'Bluejacking' is where people nearby send anonymous messages to users who have left Bluetooth switched on.

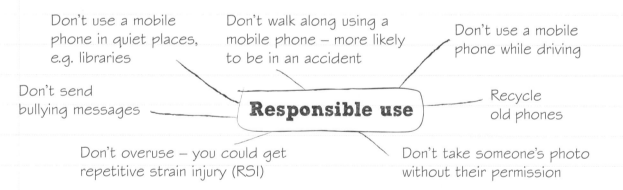

Don't use a mobile phone in quiet places, e.g. libraries

Don't walk along using a mobile phone – more likely to be in an accident

Don't use a mobile phone while driving

Don't send bullying messages

Responsible use

Recycle old phones

Don't overuse – you could get repetitive strain injury (RSI)

Don't take someone's photo without their permission

Different needs

When choosing a mobile phone you should consider:

Who is it for?	What will they use it for?	What peripherals do they want to use with it?
• a teenager • a business person • an older person • a partially-sighted person	• entertainment • business • both	• docking station • hands-free kit • Bluetooth or Wi-Fi speakers

Now try this

target
E–D

Jon is concerned about data security.
State **two** ways he can protect the information stored on his phone.   **(2 marks)**

Personal computers 1

You need to understand how to select a computer that meets the needs of a particular user or scenario based on its **functionality, weight** and **cost**.

1 Desktop computers

- Need input and output peripherals such as monitor, mouse and speakers.
- Have **hard disk drives** and **optical drives**, such as **CD** and **DVD** drives, as storage devices.
- Powerful processors.
- Good connectivity (**USB, FireWire** and **HDMI**).
- Can have **Bluetooth** and **Wi-Fi** cards fitted for **wireless** communication.
- Easy to upgrade and enhance by adding extra functions.

2 Laptop computers

- Battery powered or can use an electricity supply.
- Monitor, pointing device and webcam built in.
- Have hard disk drives and optical drives, such as CD and DVD drives, and slots for SD cards.
- Have Bluetooth and Wi-Fi built in.
- Good connectivity (USB, FireWire and HDMI).
- Less easy to dismantle and upgrade.
- **Notebooks** are similar but are even more compact.

3 Netbook computers

- **Very strong** and robust.
- **Built-in** monitor and keyboard.
- **Boot up very quickly** and can be used immediately.
- **Wi-Fi** built in for Internet connection.
- **No hard disk** or optical drives.
- Have **solid state SD cards** as storage devices (less likely to be damaged if dropped and use less power).
- Designed for using the Internet and 'cloud' computing.

4 Tablet computers

- **Very light** and portable.
- **Battery** powered.
- **Touch screen** interface.
- **Virtual**, on-screen **keyboard**.
- Bluetooth, Wi-Fi and **3G** for wireless communication.
- **Cameras** for still and moving images.
- Designed for **playing media**, Internet use and reading **ebooks**.
- Can download and run **apps** as on mobile phones.

Worked example

target F-E

Sarah has a netbook which she uses on long train journeys.

(a) Give **two** features of netbooks which make them suitable for people travelling. **(2 marks)**

   1 Light and portable.   2 Long battery life.

(b) List **two** peripherals Sarah might use when travelling by train. **(2 marks)**

   1 Flash memory stick.   2 CD ROM.

Make sure you look at the context given in the question. 'Scanner' would not be a correct response because it would not be appropriate for use on a train.

Now try this

target C-B

Give **two** benefits to a school of issuing all students with netbooks. **(2 marks)**

Personal computers 2

When you are buying a new computer it is important to consider the following **features** which will impact how much your computer weighs and costs:

Processor speed

– a quick processor means a fast computer

Sound/graphics card

– allows you to see/hear graphics, videos, music and games

Wi-Fi

– a Wi-Fi enabled computer can form part of a wireless network

RAM

– lots of RAM will let the computer support more applications

Storage capacity

– a large storage capacity means you can store more files

Number of USB ports

– many peripherals use a USB connection

Battery life

– for portable devices a long battery life means less frequent charging

---

Worked example

target G-E

Matthew is choosing a new computer. He stores and watches lots of films and music and likes to edit photographs.

State **three** features that would be especially important to him. **(3 marks)**

1 Storage capacity.

2 Sound/graphics card.

3 Processor speed.

 Other suitable answers include: screen resolution, connectivity.

Ergonomics

Another very important consideration when buying new digital equipment is whether you will be able to use it comfortably.

Ergonomics is the science of designing equipment so that it is comfortable and user-friendly.

Ergonomic design can help prevent repetitive strain injuries (RSI) and other health problems.

Health risks	Causes	Possible solutions
Eye strain	• looking at screen for too long • sunlight/artificial light shining on monitor	👍 take regular breaks away from screen 👍 adjust the screen 👍 use an antiglare screen
Repetitive strain injury (RSI)	• performing repeated actions, for example clicking the mouse	👍 use wrist rests to support your hands 👍 take breaks from repeating actions
Neck and back problems	• sitting in the wrong position • sitting in the same position for a long time	👍 change height of the chair/screen 👍 adjust the lumbar support 👍 move the computer closer or further away
Pain in knees and legs	• sitting in the wrong position • sitting in the same position for a long time	👍 adjust the chair so that your feet are flat on the ground, or use a foot rest 👍 take regular breaks to stretch your legs

---

Now try this

target E

Michael's tablet computer uses a touch screen interface instead of a keyboard and mouse. State **one** risk to Michael's health from the extended use of a touch screen interface. **(1 mark)**

Cameras and camcorders 1

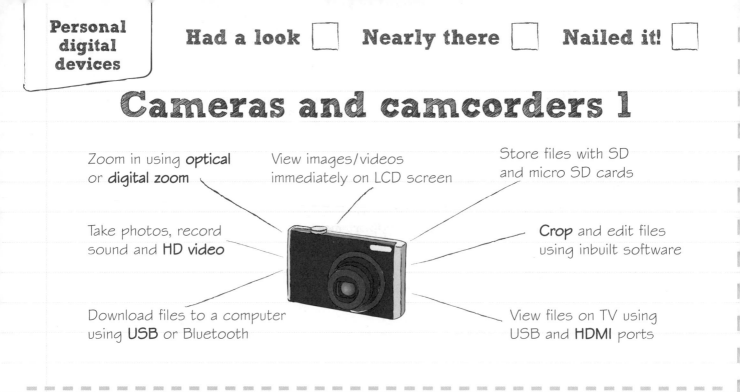

Zoom in using **optical** or **digital zoom**

View images/videos immediately on LCD screen

Store files with SD and micro SD cards

Take photos, record sound and **HD video**

Crop and edit files using inbuilt software

Download files to a computer using **USB** or Bluetooth

View files on TV using **USB** and **HDMI** ports

Digital zoom: just enlarges part of the image which can become blurred.
Optical zoom: moves the lens closer so light from the subject is brought to a focus on the sensor.

Resolution

- Images are made up of **pixels**. A pixel is a tiny point in an image. A megapixel is one million pixels.
- Generally, the more pixels, the more detailed the image so the more the image can be enlarged.
- The more pixels in an image, the larger the file size.

Worked example

Here are the specifications for two camcorders.

	Camcorder A	Camcorder B
Video format	720	1080
Zoom	digital	optical and digital
Removable storage	32 GB	2 TB
Wi-Fi	yes	no
LCD screen	yes	yes
Extra features	waterproof and shockproof GPS	none

(a) The resolution relates to the maximum number of pixels that can be recorded in the images (in the video format).

(b) Another suitable answer would be to view or use the camera's menu without having to look through the viewfinder.

target **G**

(a) Which of these camcorders has the highest resolution?   **(1 mark)**
Camcorder B.

target **G-F**

(b) Both camcorders have an LCD screen.
State two uses for the screen.   **(2 marks)**
1 To view what is being recorded.
2 To preview/review the footage.

Now try this

target **B-A**

Ciara wants to buy a new camera to photograph wildlife. She is considering a camera with a digital zoom and one with an optical zoom.
Explain why a digital zoom would not be suitable.   **(2 marks)**

Cameras and camcorders 2

More and more multifunctional devices such as mobile phones and tablets have the ability to capture images. Retailers of digital cameras have had to add new features so that people carry on buying them. You need to know about these new features.

GPS receiver

Some cameras have a GPS receiver so that the geographical coordinates can be stored in the **metadata**: the small text file stored with each image giving its details. Users can use the coordinates to see on Google Maps and Google Earth exactly where the image was taken.

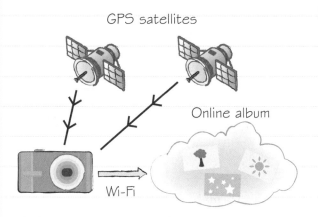

GPS satellites

Online album

Wi-Fi

Wi-Fi

Many compact digital cameras now have **Wi-Fi** connectivity in addition to cable and Bluetooth. Users can now **email** their images or **upload** them to online albums and social networking sites without the need to download the images to a computer first.

Personal camcorders

To **compete** with other devices, small, high specification personal camcorders are available. These are cheap, have a better specification than smartphones and can be used to record high definition videos. Some have Wi-Fi to allow you to upload the videos directly to Internet sites.

Now try this

target **D**

Some digital cameras now have Wi-Fi connectivity.
State **one** potential use of Wi-Fi connectivity on a digital camera.

(1 mark)

Media players 1

You need to be able to explain the features of personal media players and how they are used in different situations.

Key features

- Small, light and **easy to carry**.
- Use solid state memory so that the songs **don't 'skip'** when jolted.
- **Long battery life**.
- Hold a **lot of media** (songs, podcasts, audiobooks and videos).
- Can set **playlists**.
- Can **lock** to prevent accidental activation.
- **Simple interfaces**, e.g. jog wheel.

Media file formats

There are many file formats for audio and video.

Most **compress** the audio or video so that more can be stored on the device but this affects the quality.

Common formats include:
Audio: MP3 and WMA
Still Images: JPEG, GIF and PNG
Video: MPEG-4 and WMV

Many personal media players offer security features.

Locks automatically if it is not used for a certain period of time to prevent accidental or unauthorised use

Reactivates only when you enter the correct password or the correct **biometric authentication** for example a fingerprint

Encrypts data to prevent other people accessing it

Backup features allow users to back up their data to a computer

Uses antivirus software

Security features

Hides the Bluetooth/wireless sharing to stop users accessing files on the device

Hard reset feature allows users to delete all data from the device in the event of selling/disposing of it

Remote management (deactivation) which allows you to deactivate the device remotely if it is stolen

Now try this

Laura takes a photograph while on her run. Which of these file types would the image be stored as?   **(1 mark)**

☐ AVI   ☐ JPEG   ☐ WMV   ☐ Doc

target G

Media players 2

Digital Rights Management (DRM)

Many files include DRM software to **prevent** you from making copies of audio and video files you have downloaded on to your personal media player. The DRM software may also prevent transfer to other digital devices that you own. It is to protect the copyright holder by preventing illegal copying.

Connectivity

Wireless transfer using
• Wi-Fi
• Bluetooth
• infrared

HDMI port
• allows users to view HD movies on TV through HDMI cable

USB port
• allows transfer of files at up to 5 Gigabits per second with USB 3.0 cable

Worked example

target G–F

List **two peripherals** Emily could use with her personal media player.　　**(2 marks)**

1　Headphones.

2　Speakers.

Other possible answers are:
• docking stations
• remote control
• solar power chargers (but not mains charger because this is not a peripheral).
Pay attention to the situation being described. 'Speakers' would not be an acceptable answer if Emily was taking her media player running.

Downloading and streaming

Most users **download** audio and video files to store and play on their media players.

If the device has Wi-Fi connectivity, then the user can **stream** media. The file is sent in compressed form over the Internet and displayed by the viewer in real time.

Advantages of streaming video	Disadvantages of streaming video
👍 Saves time. A user doesn't have to wait to download a file to play it. Instead, the media is sent in a continuous stream of data and is played as it arrives by the software on the media player.	👎 Cannot keep a local copy for viewing offline.
	👎 Limited availability for some streamed video.
👍 Uses less storage space.	👎 User experience is dependent on connection quality.

Now try this

Laura has a media player with Wi-Fi connectivity and can now watch videos 'on demand'.

(a) Give **two** advantages to Laura of streaming rather than downloading videos.　　**(2 marks)**

target E–D

(b) Give **two** disadvantages to Laura of streaming rather than downloading videos.　　**(2 marks)**

target D–C

13

Games consoles 1

A video games console is a computer that enables games to be played on televisions or through digital projectors.

High resolution output for high definition games

CD, DVD and Blu-ray optical drives

Features of games consoles

Connectivity – USB, Bluetooth, Wi-Fi and Ethernet network cable

Capable of multi-player online gaming

Peripherals

- **Wireless controllers** – control the games from up to 30 feet away from the console.
- **Wireless headsets** – used to chat to other console users online.
- **Hard drive transfer cable** – to transfer games and movies to external hard disk drives.
- **Webcam/speaker/microphone set** – for video chats with other console users online.
- **Motion sensors** – for hands-free gaming.
- **High Definition** (HD) equipment for HD gaming – HD TV and HDMI cable.

Wireless and hands-free gaming

- With Nintendo Wii™ and Playstation® 3, users need to hold a **motion sensor** which has buttons for game control.
- Xbox Kinect gives 'true' **hands-free** gaming – using a laser and an infrared camera it builds up a picture of your room and works out what is a person and what is furniture. It then identifies which parts of your body are moving.

Worked example

 target **F-E**

 edexcel

Modern games consoles are **multi-functional devices**. Apart from gaming, give **two other** uses for games consoles. **(2 marks)**

1 View HD movies using Blu-ray drive.
2 Using Internet connection to stream movies.

Other possible answers include:
- Bluetooth keyboards allow consoles to be used for email and instant messaging.
- Watch digital television channels and use the console storage to pause, rewind and record programmes.

Current developments

Smart TV – also called 'connected TV' because they have an Internet connection. Used for online interactive media and on-demand film and game streaming.

Smartphones and tablets – have wired and wireless HDMI connectivity so you can use the device to play games on an HD television.

Future developments

- Controlling a game using thought alone is the aim of many developers.
- An iPhone app is available that allows users wearing a neuro headset to move and control objects on the screen using thought.

A neuro headset

Now try this

 target **D-C**

Tony is trying to decide whether to buy a computer or a dedicated games console.
(a) Give **two** advantages of buying a computer rather than a games console. **(2 marks)**
(b) Give **two** disadvantages of buying a computer rather than a games console. **(2 marks)**

Games consoles 2

You need to understand the risks of playing computer games and using games consoles.

Health risk	Causes	Prevention
Overuse injuries	pressing buttons can lead to RSI, especially of the thumbs	• set sensible time limits • take frequent breaks to stretch and flex • don't use the same controller all the time
Obesity	the amount of time spent playing computer games and obesity are linked	• set sensible time limits • do physical activities when not playing
Muscle and joint problems	hours in the same position impacts on posture and spine	• take regular breaks to walk around and stretch • adjust the furniture to suit your height • use an ergonomic chair if possible
Eye strain	eyes become fatigued when focused at the same distance point for long periods: symptoms include blurry vision and headaches	• adjust the screen for contrast and brightness • move furniture so that light doesn't shine on the screen • take 'gaze' breaks: look at objects in the distance

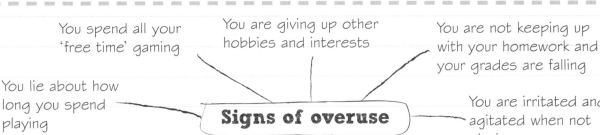

You spend all your 'free time' gaming

You are giving up other hobbies and interests

You are not keeping up with your homework and your grades are falling

You lie about how long you spend playing

Signs of overuse

You are irritated and agitated when not playing games

You would rather play games than spend time with family and friends

When you are sad or upset you escape into a game

Worked example

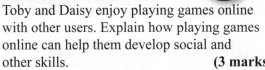

target D-B

Toby and Daisy enjoy playing games online with other users. Explain how playing games online can help them develop social and other skills. **(3 marks)**

Playing games online with other people gives them the opportunity to play in a team with other people. They can chat with other players and encourage or praise them. It gives them the opportunity to meet players from all around the world and learn about different cultures.

Effects on behaviour

- A report suggested that exposure to violent video games causes aggression and decreases empathy (feelings) for others.
- Brain scans have shown that playing a shooting game for 10 hours in a week results in less brain activity in regions involving thinking and emotional control.

For these reasons:

- Governments have passed laws regulating, prohibiting or banning violent games.
- Video games are classified in the same way as films.

Now try this

target C-A*

*Some people claim that playing video games is beneficial. Make a reasoned argument to support this point of view.

(6 marks)

The asterisk means that the quality of your written communication will be assessed.

Home entertainment systems

Home entertainment systems are designed to provide **high quality audio and video throughout a house** and to **integrate** the content on separate digital devices.

Digital television

- **More channels** than analogue TV.
- **High quality** pictures and sound.
- **Digital radio stations** accessible on TV.
- The **electronic programme guide** (EPG) displays programme information on-screen.

- More **accessible**: subtitles, audio and sign language descriptions.
- **Interactive features** e.g. extra coverage, voting and shopping capabilities.
- **Greater control**: save programmes and pause live TV.

Worked example

List **two** ways in which digital television signals can be delivered to the home. **(2 marks)**

1 By cable.
2 By satellite.

Internet

Smart TVs and games consoles allow users to stream channels or films directly from the Internet.

Apple TV also allows users to access the audio and video media stored in their **iCloud**.

Enhancements

- **Digital projectors** project HD images from a computer, set top box, personal media player or DVD/Blu-ray player on to a screen or wall.
- **Home cinema / theatre systems** include DVD/Blu-ray player, amplifier and six speakers to provide high-fidelity surround sound.

Personal video recorders (PVR) or digital video recorders (DVR) contain a **hard disk drive** allowing you to **record** TV programmes.

Set top boxes transform and enhance the signal from the cable or satellite to a form that the TV can display.

Blu-ray players play HD movies on Blu-ray discs (which can store up to 50 GB).

Integration

As home Wi-Fi networks become more common, people are now able to integrate their media devices.

For example, you can access your entire CD collection in every room via a music server with the actual album cover art displayed on a touch panel.

Digital Living Network Alliance (DLNA)

If two devices are DLNA certified, then they are compatible straight out of the box. So you can access content from your PC, camera or smartphone on your TV, or play music from your personal media player through your Hi-Fi without plugging anything in or transferring files between devices.

Now try this

Some friends wirelessly display images from their phones on their television. Describe how they might do this. **(3 marks)**

Satellite navigation 1

You need to understand how personal digital devices use GPS to plan routes and give directions.

Worked example

edexcel ⠿

target
E

State the function of GPS.   **(1 mark)**
Global Positioning System (GPS) gives you an accurate location of where you are by receiving signals from a network of satellites.

EXAM ALERT!

About half of students got this question wrong. GPS just tells you where you are. Giving directions is a function of navigation devices.

This was a real exam question that a lot of students struggled with – **be prepared!**   ResultsPlus

Satellite navigation systems

Satellite navigation systems (sat navs) use GPS to plan routes and give directions. Sat navs are used by drivers, pedestrians and geocachers.

Drivers

In addition to route planning, drivers use sat navs to:

- **check their speed** and warn them about **speed cameras**
- get live **traffic reports** and **avoid congestion**
- find scenic routes or **conveniences**, such as service stations.

Health and safety risks

- Driver may take eyes off the road / cause an accident while trying to adjust settings / route.
- Device may cause a 'blind spot'.
- Device could lead driver down hard-to-navigate roads or to incorrect destinations.

Worked example

target **D**

Sally uses her sat nav when travelling to see relations who live a long way away. State how bookmarking a location in a sat nav can help her.
    (1 mark)

It saves her time typing in the address or searching for it every time she visits.

If an answer is 'easier', 'quicker' or 'saves time', then remember to say why, otherwise you might not gain the mark.

Pedestrians

Pedestrians can use sat navs to find their way in cities or in the countryside. Pedestrian sat navs are small waterproof, shockproof devices that give geographical coordinates and contain a compass.

Geocaching

Geocaching is an outdoor, high-tech **treasure hunt**. Players try to locate hidden containers, called geocaches, using GPS-enabled devices and then share their experiences online.

Now try this

target **D**

target **D–C**

(a) When Shameela drives through a road tunnel she notices that the display on her sat nav freezes. State what might have caused this.   **(1 mark)**

(b) Describe **one** health and safety risk of using a sat nav while driving.   **(2 marks)**

Satellite navigation 2

Convergence

Convergence is where digital devices take on functions **normally found in other devices**. GPS and sat nav functions are now offered on a variety of devices:

- smartphones and media players now have GPS receivers and free downloadable maps

- route planning apps are available for smartphones.

Sales of dedicated sat navs are falling so some sat nav manufacturers now produce their own apps for smartphones.

Dedicated sat nav manufacturers are responding by producing sat navs with new features:

- larger screens
- 3D displays
- lane assist with images of actual junctions
- Bluetooth links to mobile phones so they can be used for voice calls
- eco-route planning to save petrol on journeys.

Dedicated sat nav or smartphone app?

Advantages of using a smartphone

👍 You are always likely to have your **mobile phone with you** so you will always have your sat nav with you.

👍 They are generally **small, light** and easy to carry around.

👍 If you already own a smartphone, then you can buy **applications** from the major sat nav manufacturers for your phone.

Disadvantages of using a smartphone

👎 You might have to pay for an **expensive** sat nav app if your phone does not come with one.

👎 You can be subject to **charges** if you do not have a good deal on your mobile Internet usage and you will have to pay roaming charges if you use it abroad.

👎 Using GPS on your mobile phone **runs the battery down** quickly.

👎 Smartphone sat nav **does not always update quickly** enough, which could cause you to miss instructions.

Worked example

target F-E

State **two** reasons why Molly might want to buy an SD card for her sat nav. **(2 marks)**

1 She wants to update the maps she has already.
2 She has run out of space to store extra maps.

Some sat navs let you play music through them so you could also have said 'She wants to play music on her sat nav'.

Accessibility

- Some sat navs provide extra information for people with disabilities, such as the location of dedicated disabled parking areas. They also provide local information for those with disabilities about disabled toilets and facilities in shops, train stations and other public places.
- Sat navs for blind people will speak their location at the press of a button.

Now try this

target E-D

Give **two** advantages of using a sat nav rather than printed instructions. **(2 marks)**

Impact on organisations

The use of digital devices has affected the ways in which all organisations operate.

Organisations use computers for **storing data**, **design tasks**, **production tasks** (e.g. computer-controlled machines), **planning**, **advertising** and **communicating**.

Computers

The introduction of computers has had an impact on:

- the number of employees needed
- the skills employees need
- training and re-training requirements.

Portable digital devices

Many organisations issue their employees with portable digital devices (e.g. **mobile phones**, **laptops**, **netbooks** and **tablets**) and make remote access possible through **wireless** and **3G networks** and by storing data and files in a 'cloud'.

👍 Allows **greater collaboration** between workers at different sites.

👎 Puts organisations at greater risk of **hackers stealing or corrupting data**.

Online presence

As more of their customers use digital devices, organisations need a strong online presence:

- **website** – to showcase goods and services and **sell online**
- **blog** – to tell customers about developments in a more personal way
- presence on **social networking sites** – to monitor comments and engage in discussions
- **viral marketing** – to advertise their services through video uploads
- **profiling** – tracking information about customer transactions gathered using cookies.

Worked example

target
C-A

Tina is a sales rep who travels most of the week. Explain how she might use her smartphone to communicate with people while travelling.

(3 marks)

She can use Bluetooth to allow her to speak to customers while driving. She can use 3G or Wi-Fi when in a hotel/meeting to email/chat/text with colleagues.

Internet allows better online **research**

Laptops, netbooks and smartphones allow access to online learning resources

Apps for smartphones and tablets make learning more enjoyable

Interactive whiteboards, digital cameras and devices with GPS enhance the learning experience

Technology in education

VLEs allow access to learning resources and let students hand in homework any time

Specialist software improves learning in certain subjects, e.g. languages

Online registration and admin systems for schools improve efficiency

Ebook readers give better access to lots of texts

Now try this

target
E-C

List **three** positive effects of the use of digital devices in education.   **(3 marks)**

Had a look ☐ Nearly there ☐ Nailed it! ☐

Home networks

Most homes with a **home network** use it primarily to allow users to **share** an **Internet connection**. You need to know how to set up a network and the types of network available.

Local area network

To create a home network you need to set up a **local area network** or **LAN**. This connects all the computers in the house so that resources can be shared. Benefits of a home network include:

- sharing the Internet connection
- sharing files, including backing up files
- sharing peripherals, for example printers
- Internet telephone services.

You need a **network interface card (NIC)** to connect the computers to the network unless you are using Wi-Fi dongles.

Routers

Connecting to the Internet from a home network requires a router. The **router** connects all of the computers to the modem by giving them an internal **IP address** so that it 'knows' where to send the data. Most Internet Service Providers will give you a modem and router combined.

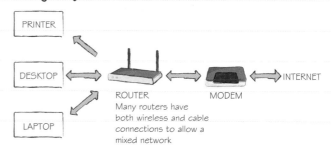

PRINTER

DESKTOP

LAPTOP

ROUTER   MODEM   INTERNET

Many routers have both wireless and cable connections to allow a mixed network

Types of network

	Cable connection to router using Ethernet cable or CAT5 cable	Wireless (Wi-Fi or wireless Ethernet) connection to router using radio waves or microwaves
Setting up	cables have to be run from the router to all rooms in the house	all you need is a wireless router
Cost	installation is expensive	cheaper: only the cost of the router
Bandwidth	very fast: 1 Gigabit per second (Gbps). NICs are very cheap	slower: 54 Megabits per second (Mbps). New standards achieve up to 300 Mbps
Security	good: a user would need to physically plug their computer into the network with a cable	poor: anyone within range can use it unless kept secure with a security password or key
Interference	should not experience interference	can be affected by walls, electronic equipment, distance from router and number of computers connected
Mobility	you cannot connect in a room without a socket. You have to unplug and reconnect if you want to move to a different room	you can access the network from anywhere in the house and you can stay connected moving from room to room

Another means of connection is **Powerline**. A Powerline network (for example HomePlug Powerline Alliance) uses existing power wiring as a framework to carry data.

Now try this

target F-E

(a) Give **two** benefits of using a wireless network in the home. **(2 marks)**

target E

(b) State what piece of equipment needs to be connected to the modem in order to share the connection over a wireless network.

(1 mark)

Network security

Wireless networks are **less secure** than cable ones. If you do not secure your wireless network then anyone within **range** can access it.

Worked example

edexcel

Lee sees this pop up when he tries to connect to the wireless network.

target E-C

The pop up displays the names of the wireless networks.
Explain what else it tells Lee about these wireless networks.   **(3 marks)**

- Some of the wireless networks are secured and some are non-secured.
- Signal strength of the networks is displayed as bars.
- Type of encryption used, for example WPA and WPA2.

The importance of security

When you connect to your own wireless network you will probably see all of the others within range in a pop up like this one. Just as you can see other people's networks, they can see yours and, if it is not secure, they will be able to use your Internet connection – at your cost. Even if you trust your neighbours there are websites which publish the location of unsecured 'hot spots' so that people can get Internet access without paying.

Other correct answers:
- you cannot access the secured networks unless you have the key
- your data is at risk if you use a non-secured network
- the signal strength will affect the performance of the connection
- the routers are broadcasting their SSID.

Ways of securing wireless networks

- Changing the default admin password on the router.
- Setting up a form of **encryption**.
- Setting up **Media Access Control (MAC)** address filtering.
- Hiding the router by stopping the router broadcasting its **Service Set Identifier (SSID)**.
- Turning off the router when it is not in use.
- Reducing transmitter power.

- **Encryption** scrambles data so that only computers with the right key can read it. The commonest form of protection for wireless networks is WEP, but WPA-PSK and WPA2 are more secure and are becoming more popular.
- Each device in your network has a **MAC** address. You can specify which addresses can connect to your wireless network.
- Remember that a firewall or physically locking the door will not prevent people accessing a non-secure wireless network.

Now try this

(a) State **two** ways to secure a wireless network.   **(2 marks)**

(b) Explain why it is important to secure a wireless network.   **(2 marks)**

Combining technologies

You can achieve a lot more with digital devices by **using them together**. You need to be able to describe how digital devices are **compatible** with each other.

Communications technologies in different devices

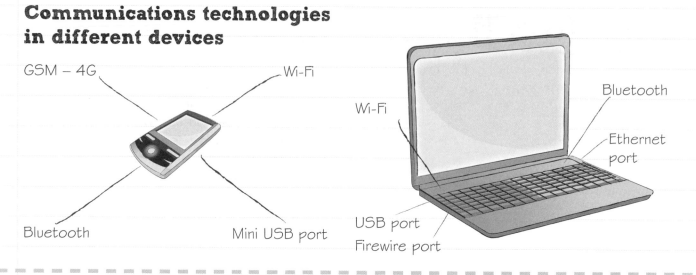

GSM – 4G

Wi-Fi

Bluetooth

Mini USB port

Wi-Fi

Bluetooth

Ethernet port

USB port
Firewire port

Communications technologies working together

The mobile phone and the laptop above are **compatible** because they both have USB ports, and can communicate via Wi-Fi or Bluetooth technology. So you could use the camera on the mobile phone to take a photograph, transfer it to a memory stick and then send via Ethernet cable.

Many digital devices are **converging**: performing functions that were originally performed by different devices. If your mobile phone has a camera and an Internet connection, you could take and upload photos to a website using just that one device. A device that can perform several functions is called a **multifunctional device**.

Worked example

target C-B

Jill wears a headset when driving so that she can make calls hands free. State **two** wireless communication networks that enable her to do this. **(2 marks)**

1   Bluetooth

2   3G

Now try this

Jack is travelling through Europe and would like to upload images he has taken to online albums. He has a digital camera, a mobile phone and a netbook.

target E-D

(a) List **two** ways in which he could transfer the images from his camera to his netbook. **(2 marks)**

target C-B

(b) Jack is in an area where there is no Wi-Fi signal.
Describe how Jack could upload the images from his netbook. **(2 marks)**

Bandwidth and latency

Using a network connection involves transferring **bits** (1s and 0s) between two devices. **Network performance** is how well that network can transfer the bits. **Bandwidth** and **latency** are two measurements to describe the performance of a network connection.

Bandwidth: measurement of capacity

Bandwidth is the number of bits that can go through the network connection in 1 second. It is measured in **bits per second** (bps).

1 Kbps means 1 thousand bits can be transmitted every second

1 Mbps means 1 million bits can be transmitted every second

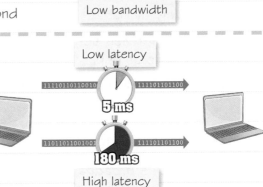

High bandwidth

Low bandwidth

Latency: measurement of delay

Latency is the time in milliseconds between a bit leaving one device and arriving at the other. It is measured in **milliseconds** (ms).

Low latency

5 ms

180 ms

High latency

User experience

For **streaming** videos from YouTube you need a high bandwidth network connection, otherwise the video will keep pausing as your computer waits for more bits to arrive.

To get quick search results from Google you need a low latency network connection. Information is travelling in both directions so it needs to arrive quickly.

> The best networks, including those suitable for online gaming, have high bandwidth and low latency. Remember that low bandwidth and high latency are usually bad from a user's point of view.

Downloading lots of files at once will slow down data transfer as the bandwith is being shared by each download. Students often get confused and think other tasks (e.g. using a word processor or media

Worked example

target **F**

Nisha is choosing a new broadband supplier. She compared four different suppliers.

Supplier	Download speed
SpeedLine	2 Mbps
ACE Broadband	1 Mbps
Quickweb	16 Mbps
DataDudes	8 Mbps

Which **one** of these suppliers offers the best bandwidth? **(1 mark)**

A SpeedLine ☐

B ACE Broadband ☐

C Quickweb ☒

D DataDudes ☐

player) will also slow down data transfer, but this is not the case.

> Students have struggled with exam questions similar to this – **be prepared!**

target **C-B**

Jed wants to watch BBC iPlayer in HD on his computer. Explain why the bandwidth of Jed's Internet connection is important. **(2 marks)**

For both marks you need to explain what bandwidth is **and** why it is important.

Wi-Fi and mobile broadband

The most common ways of connecting to the Internet on the move are **Wi-Fi hotspots** and **mobile broadband** which relies on the **3G** network at present.

Wi-Fi

Wi-Fi devices need to be within range of a wireless access point or '**hotspot**'.

Wireless Access Point

- 👍 **Good range** – works up to 60 metres from the hotspot.
- 👍 **Speeds** of up to 54 Mbps.
- 👍 Quite widely available.
- 👎 **Hackers** sometimes set up fake Wi-Fi hotspots putting users' details at risk.
- 👎 Cannot use if **not in range** of an access point.

Mobile broadband

At present, mobile broadband allows devices to connect to the Internet via the same network that 3G mobile phones use. Many mobile phones have the technology to pick up 3G signals built in, whereas other devices such as laptops need a **dongle**. A mobile phone with 3G capability can also be made into a hotspot.

- 👍 Far **greater coverage** than Wi-Fi.
- 👍 **More secure** than Wi-Fi – data is encrypted.
- 👎 Have to **pay** for mobile broadband, including **roaming charges** if you are abroad.
- 👎 **Downloads limited**.
- 👎 **Lower bandwidth** than Wi-Fi.

Worked example

edexcel

target **D-C**

State **one** benefit and **one** limitation of mobile broadband. **(2 marks)**

Benefit: It can be used anywhere there is a signal.

Limitation: There is usually a download limit.

EXAM ALERT!

Students tended to muddle 'mobile broadband' and broadband available on a mobile phone.

This was a real exam question that a lot of students struggled with – **be prepared!**

ResultsPlus

Now try this

target **D-B**

Caroline is touring Europe and needs to use her laptop to access the Internet to keep in touch with family and to upload photos. Explain the benefits of using Wi-Fi rather than her 3G dongle. **(3 marks)**

This question asks you to **explain**. You are being asked to compare Wi-Fi with 3G so make sure you mention both in your answer.

Peer-to-peer networks

A peer-to-peer network is when digital devices **communicate wirelessly** with each other **directly** without the need for a transmitter between them. You need to know about the technology that allows **peer-to-peer networks** to be set up.

In the past...

Devices communicated with each other through a transmitter: a wireless access point when using Wi-Fi and a mobile phone mast when using mobile broadband.

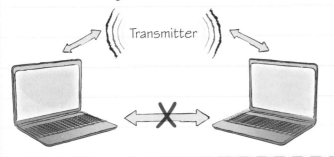

Transmitter

Wi-Fi Direct

The Wi-Fi Alliance has now introduced Wi-Fi Direct. This new technology allows devices to connect directly using Wi-Fi **without the need for a wireless access point**.

👍 Wi-Fi Direct allows users to set up peer-to-peer networks.

👍 Wi-Fi Direct also allows the devices to use an access point for normal Wi-Fi use.

Bluetooth

Another way of establishing a peer-to-peer network is to use Bluetooth.

👍 Allows devices to communicate **automatically** when within range – with no user involvement.

👍 Can connect up to **eight devices** at the same time.

👍 **Low power** so does not interfere with other devices.

Bluetooth 4 versus Wi-Fi Direct

	Bluetooth 4	Wi-Fi Direct
Bandwidth	25 Mbps	250 Mbps
Range	60 metres	200 metres

Worked example

target C-B

(a) Explain why Bluetooth rather than traditional Wi-Fi is used for communication between a mobile phone and a headset for hands-free phone calls.　**(2 marks)**

Using Bluetooth, the two devices can communicate directly without the need for a transmitter. They can also communicate automatically without the need for any user actions.

target B-A

(b) Give **two** reasons to why Bluetooth is not used to network devices in a large office.
　(2 marks)

Bluetooth has a lower range so the devices being networked need to be close together, which would not be the case in a large office. It has a low bandwidth and so data transfer would be slow.

Part (a) is asking for an advantage of using Bluetooth to connect a mobile phone and a hands-free device so saying 'It can connect up to eight devices at once' isn't a valid response.

Now try this

target C-B

Some newspaper articles have claimed that Wi-Fi Direct will replace Bluetooth in most digital devices. List **two** reasons why this could be the case.　**(2 marks)**

Communication protocols 1

Protocols are the rules that devices must follow when they are communicating with each other. You need to know about **VoIP**, **POP**, **IMAP** and **SMTP**.

VoIP

- **Voice over Internet Protocol** is the set of rules for transmitting audio messages over the Internet. The rules enable you to make **free voice calls** from your computer to your friends' computers. It is particularly useful for keeping in touch when travelling or with someone who is travelling.
- If you use a webcam as well, then you can make **video calls**.
- You can even use VoIP from a smartphone.

This student has rightly identified the **equipment** as the question asked them to. Although you also need an Internet connection and software, such as Skype, to make VoIP calls, these answers wouldn't have been appropriate here.

Worked example

target G–F

Layla would like to use VoIP on her netbook to keep in touch with her cousin in Canada.

(a) State **two** pieces of equipment she will need to make calls. **(2 marks)**

1   A microphone.

2   Headphones or speakers.

target D

(b) Most of Layla's friends have computers at home. She finds that she cannot use VoIP to call some of them. Give **one** possible reason for this. **(1 mark)**

Layla's friends' computers might not be set up for VoIP.

POP3, IMAP and SMTP

POP3, IMAP and SMTP are all communication protocols used when sending and receiving emails.

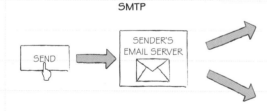

SMTP

SEND → SENDER'S EMAIL SERVER → RECIPIENT'S EMAIL SERVER

POP takes the email from the server and delivers it to the recipient's computer → RECIPIENT'S COMPUTER

RECIPIENT'S EMAIL SERVER

IMAP keeps the email on the server

Simple Mail Transfer Protocol (SMTP) is used when email is sent from the sender's email client, for example Outlook, to the sender's email server and when the email is delivered to the recipient's email server.

If the recipient uses **Post Office Protocol (POP or POP3)** to read the email, the mail server will **download the email** to the computer. The email is then **deleted from the server** and can be read offline.

If the recipient uses **Internet Message Access Protocol (IMAP)**, the email is read on **the mail server**. The email is not deleted from the server and can be accessed anywhere using any computer with an Internet connection.

Now try this

target B–A

John's email account uses the POP protocol. Describe how the POP protocol is different from IMAP when retrieving an email. **(2 marks)**

Communication protocols 2

You need to know about the communication protocols used to surf the Internet (**HTTP**) and send confidential information (**HTTPS**).

HTTP

Hypertext Transfer Protocol (**HTTP**) is the protocol of the **World Wide Web** (WWW).

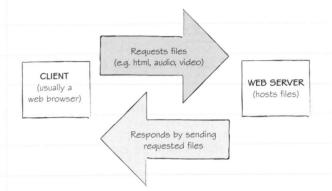

When you type in a website address the **client** (your browser) uses HTTP to ask the **web server** to send the files needed to show the web page on your computer.

HTTPS

When sending confidential information over the Internet the web server uses a protocol called **Hypertext Transfer Protocol over SSL (Secure Sockets Layer)** or HTTPS. The data transferred is **encrypted** so that it cannot be read by anyone except the recipient.

When the HTTPS protocol is being used the URL should show in the address bar as **https://**

Depending on the browser you are using, the padlock icon may appear.

Digital certificates

If you double-click the padlock icon or security icon you will see the website's **digital certificate**.

These digital certificates are issued by companies such as Norton. They certify the identity of the website your browser is communicating with. But beware: these certificates can be faked so study them carefully.

How HTTPS works

1. The browser checks the site's certificate.
2. The web server and your browser determine the encryption types that they can both use to understand each other.
3. Your browser and the web server send each other unique codes to use when encrypting the information being sent.
4. Your browser and the web server start talking to each other using the encryption.

Worked example

edexcel

Explain how encryption helps to keep data secure.   **(2 marks)**

Encryption turns data into a secret code using a key. Only someone with the key can read the data.

EXAM ALERT!

Only a fifth of students gained full marks on this question. Make sure you understand encryption and how authorised users can decrypt the message.

This was a real exam question that a lot of students struggled with – **be prepared!**

Now try this

target **F**

Which one of these protocols would be used to upload a podcast to a blog?   **(1 mark)**

☐ HTTP   ☐ SMS   ☐ POP   ☐ IMAP

Security risks in a network

When you connect to a computer network there are **security risks** to be aware of. You need to know about the **digital** security risks and how to **reduce** and **overcome** them.

Remote access

When you connect a computer to a network it is visible to all the other computers on the network. When you connect to the Internet your computer is visible to billions of computers around the world. You can prevent remote access to your computer with a **firewall**.

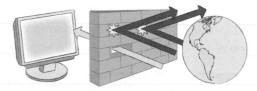

A firewall is software that **permits or blocks connections** between your computer and other computers on the network according to the rules you have set. A firewall is not enough on its own because some **malware**, such as a virus, works by shutting down your firewall.

A virus is a program designed to cause other computer programs to malfunction or stop working. Viruses can replicate themselves and can be passed on to other users in files and emails.

Additional precautions to take against viruses:

- install antivirus software and keep it updated
- run regular scans of files on the computer
- only download from trusted websites
- only open emails and attachments from recognised senders
- scan CDs, DVDs and memory sticks before accessing them
- do not use pirate copies of CDs and DVDs
- avoid file-sharing websites.

Intercepting data

Users send sensitive personal information across networks (including the Internet) such as:

- credit card information
- personal details
- sensitive company information
- bank account information.

This information can be intercepted and read by other network users who may use it to commit fraud. **Encryption** is one way of keeping data safe.

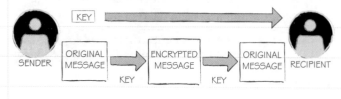

Illegal access

Data can be stolen or corrupted by unauthorised users on a network. **Authentication** – the process of identifying an individual – can prevent illegal access.

Most networks require a user to have a **username** and a **password** in order to prove their identity. The user may be required to select a **strong** password consisting of:

- numbers
- upper case and lower case letters
- punctuation marks.

To ensure that the user is human, and not a computer program, they may be given a **captcha test**. For more information on captcha tests, see page 33.

Now try this

target **C-B**   **(a)** Explain why firewalls are used by people when accessing the Internet. **(2 marks)**

target **D-C**   **(b)** Data can be encrypted when it is sent to other people over the Internet. Explain how encryption helps keep data secure. **(2 marks)**

Physical security risks

As well as digital security risks, there are physical risks to your equipment and your data. You need to know about the physical risks and how to prevent them.

Physical access to data

Data is at risk from people physically accessing your computer and stealing it.

	Help and Support
All Programs	
Start Search 🔍 ⏻ 🔒 ▸	
	Lock this computer

When leaving your computer unattended you can use the **'Lock' function** in Windows so that a password is required to start using it again.

Preventing theft of equipment

Chains and locks can be used to fix a desktop computer or a laptop to a desk. Having locks on doors and blinds on windows are other simple ways of keeping equipment safe.

Radio Frequency Identification (RFID) chips can be used in labels attached to items. A scanner can read the chip and identify the product. It could also sound an alarm if the item is being taken out of a building or shop.

For companies who have many computers installed together in large network rooms there are several strategies that can be used to physically prevent unauthorised users from accessing the computers and data.

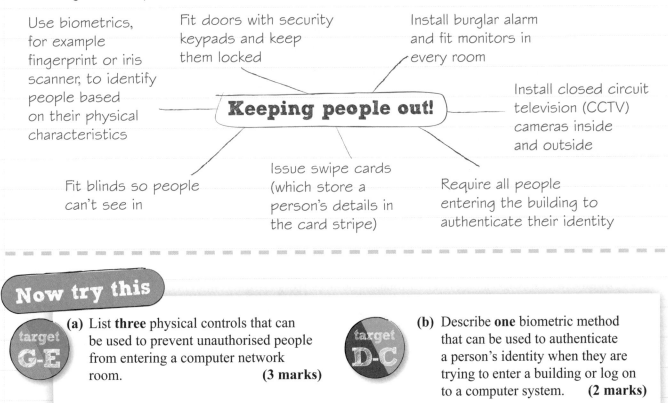

Use biometrics, for example fingerprint or iris scanner, to identify people based on their physical characteristics

Fit doors with security keypads and keep them locked

Install burglar alarm and fit monitors in every room

Install closed circuit television (CCTV) cameras inside and outside

Keeping people out!

Fit blinds so people can't see in

Issue swipe cards (which store a person's details in the card stripe)

Require all people entering the building to authenticate their identity

Now try this

target G-E

(a) List **three** physical controls that can be used to prevent unauthorised people from entering a computer network room. **(3 marks)**

target D-C

(b) Describe **one** biometric method that can be used to authenticate a person's identity when they are trying to enter a building or log on to a computer system. **(2 marks)**

The Internet

You need to be able to describe how users can connect to the Internet.

What is the Internet?

The Internet is a **huge network** that links networks of computers all over the world. All of the computers use the **same protocol** – TCP/IP – so that they can communicate and send data to each other.

One of the most widely used services on the Internet is the World Wide Web (WWW) which uses the HTTP protocol to allow users to access the interlinked hypertext documents that we call web pages.

To connect to the Internet you need a **network interface card** (NIC) to get a cable or Wi-Fi connection. You also need to sign up with an Internet Service Provider (ISP).

Wi-Fi Switch—
Ethernet Port—

Selecting an ISP – things to consider

Cost	ISPs charge a monthly fee and there may be a set-up cost
Bandwidth	This varies widely. Usually the higher the bandwidth, the higher the fee. The figure ISPs advertise is a maximum usually never reached because of other network traffic (contention)
Download limits	Some ISPs impose a limit on what you can download in a month. They charge extra if you go over the limit
Email and web space	Most ISPs will give you email addresses and provide space on their servers for you to create your own website
Security	Broadband, always-on, connections are vulnerable to hackers. The ISP should provide you with a firewall, antivirus and antispam software, and parental controls
Reliability and support	Some ISPs never provide the bandwidth they promise and have very poor customer care. You can check magazines, online forums and user groups for advice

Worked example

edexcel

Here is a list of ISPs and the services they offer:

	Suppliers			
	FastWeb	**BB Broadband**	**Lime Mobile**	**JetNetz**
Download speed	20 mbps	8 mbps	6 mbps	30 mbps
Monthly usage	250 GB	Unlimited	15 GB	100 GB

target **G**

(a) Which ISP offers the best bandwidth? **(1 mark)**

JetNetz: high bandwidth means faster data flow.

target **E**

(b) BB Broadband offers '**unlimited**' monthly usage. State what this means. **(1 mark)**

There is no cap so you can download as much data as you want each month.

Now try this

target **D-B**

List **three** things to consider when looking for a new ISP. **(3 marks)**

Internet use 1

The widespread use of the Internet has had a huge effect on the ways in which individuals and societies live. You should be able to discuss how the Internet is used in all areas of life.

Email
- Sending messages
- Can access using laptops, mobile phones, tablets and so on

Instant messaging (IM)
- 'Talking' in real time by typing messages
- Helps **collaboration**

Blogs
- Shared online diaries
- Post and share experiences
- Twitter is a microblog (you can only post 140 characters)

Communicating on the Internet

Online albums
- Photo albums hosted on a website
- Allows you to share and back up photos

Voice over Internet Protocol (VoIP)
- Need fast Internet connection
- Example: Skype

Social networking
- Websites that allow chat, messaging, email, groups and file sharing
- Examples: Facebook, MySpace, Bebo

I use the Internet to:
- keep in touch with friends through email and social networking sites
- download and stream music and films
- keep up to date with news through RSS feeds
- access my school's VLE.

Privacy

When communicating online it is important to protect your personal information. You can use account settings on social networking sites to restrict who can see your personal details, photos and posts.

---

 target C-B

edexcel

Explain how having access to the Internet could enhance a family's daily life. **(3 marks)**

Having access to the Internet can enhance the family's daily life in many ways. They could use the Internet to help with learning and school work because it gives you access to countless types of information. They could use the Internet to teach themselves by using sites such as BBC bitesize. The family could also use the Internet to shop online and make payments online – this is more convenient than going to the shops. It also allows them to compare prices online. The family could also use the Internet to research travel arrangements (for example booking holidays). Socialising online allows them to keep in touch with distant relatives and friends regularly.

This student has made a range of points and would gain full marks. When asked to 'explain' you cannot simply list points. You must explain each point that you make as this student has done.

Now try this

 target D-C

Identify **two** advantages of using social networking technology rather than SMS to communicate with friends. **(2 marks)**

Take care – don't lose marks for just saying 'cheaper' and 'quicker' without really thinking about the question.

Internet use 2

You should be able to discuss how the Internet is used in business and learning.

Business on the Internet

Business tool	Description	Pros and cons
Email Instant messaging VoIP	ways of communicating over the Internet	👍 aid **collaboration** 👎 possibility of over-reliance or misuse
Cloud computing	storing software and data centrally so it can be accessed anywhere	👍 don't need to buy multiple software licences 👎 possible security issues with data stored by third party
Video conferencing	two-way audio and video transmissions	👍 reduces need for travel so lowers costs 👎 people don't communicate as well as when face to face

Virtual Learning Environment (VLE)

web-based system allowing students, parents and teachers to communicate in a 'virtual school'

👍 students can access tasks and resources uploaded by teachers, and track progress

👎 cannot access if you do not have an Internet connection

News websites

👍 can use RSS feeds to see latest stories

👍 can search archives to find old stories

👎 possible over-reliance on news websites rather than using a number of sources for research

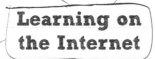

Learning on the Internet

User-generated websites (WIKIs)

websites to which people can add their own content

👍 up-to-date information source which draws on lots of people's knowledge and expertise

👎 anyone can add content so information may be **inaccurate** or **biased**

Email, instant messaging, VoIP

👍 improved / quicker communication

👎 possible over-reliance / overuse

Worked example

Harry uses the school VLE to check his timetable at home.

target D-C

(a) Describe **one** other way in which the VLE can help Harry with his school work. **(2 marks)**

Harry can upload his homework to the VLE which means he will never forget to take his homework to school.

target E-D

(b) State **two** drawbacks of relying on the VLE. **(2 marks)**

If Harry does not have a suitable home computer, he will be unable to use the VLE. Also, if he experiences technical problems with the computer or the network he will be unable to use it.

Now try this

target C-A

Explain how the widespread use of the Internet has had an impact on:
(a) how people communicate with each other. **(3 marks)**
(b) the number of people who work from home. **(3 marks)**

 Remember – the command word is 'explain'. Each of your points should have an explanation.

Security measures

Sometimes when you log into a site you are asked to change your password. Passwords should be at least six characters long and should not contain spaces.

target G-F

(a) Identify **two** other features of a strong password. **(2 marks)**

Use something that will not be easily guessed, that is, do not use a name or date of birth. Use a mixture of numbers, letters and symbols.

target F-E

(b) List **two** things you must do to keep your password secure. **(2 marks)**

1 Do not write it down.
2 Change it regularly.

EXAM ALERT!

Make sure you are giving two **different** answers. 'Include lowercase letters' and 'Include uppercase letters' are really the same thing.

Students have struggled with exam questions similar to this – **be prepared!**

ResultsPlus

Usernames and passwords

When you buy goods online or join a social networking site you will have to set up an account and in future log in with a **username** and **password**.

You use the password to **authenticate** – to prove your identity.

Part **(a)** is asking for features of a strong password. The following answer could also have been given:

- Use a mix of upper and lower case letters.

Part **(b)** is asking about keeping the password secure. The following answers could also have been given:

- Do not tell anyone your password.
- Do not allow anyone to watch you type it in.
- Avoid allowing browsers to remember the password on shared / public PCs.
- Use different passwords for different sites.
- Encrypt passwords.

Security questions

Security questions are one example of a **challenge-response** test. When you set up an account you will be asked to select a security question and to enter your own 'secret answer'.

Question:	Select one ▾
Secret answer:	Select one
	Mother's birthplace
	Best childhood friend
	Name of first pet
First name:	Favorite teacher
	Favorite historical person
Last name:	Grandfather's occupation

If you forget your password you can use your secret answer to verify your identity. More about secret answers

Some sites, such as banks, require you to answer security questions as well as entering your password.

You can also answer your secret question to identify yourself if you have forgotten your password.

Proving that you are human!

When you create accounts online you may be given a challenge-response test called a **captcha** where you have to enter the letters and numbers shown.

Characters: [   ]

Enter the 8 characters you see

This is done to check that the form is not being completed automatically by a software program known as a 'bot' or 'web robot'.

There is no software that can read the letters displayed and enter them into the required field. Captchas are used to protect systems vulnerable to email spam.

Now try this

target D-C

(a) Describe how security questions can be used for authentication when users are logging into an online account. **(2 marks)**

target E

(b) (i) State what a Captcha test is. **(1 mark)**
(ii) Explain why they are used. **(2 marks)**

target D-C

Personal spaces

Many people have a personal presence on the Internet. You need to know about the responsibilities and risks involved in having personal web space.

personal websites   online photo albums   forums

Types of personal spaces — blogs

personal page on VLE/work social media platforms   social networking sites

Personalise your space

You can design your own websites and blogs. You can also personalise your social networking and personal VLE pages.

You can add:

- photos
- personal information
- text and weblinks
- likes and dislikes
- news feeds.

You need to be careful because what you publish tells the world what you are like!

Worked example

Many people give away personal information on social networking sites. Give **one** way that social networking sites might be sharing information about you.　**(1 mark)**

The sites might allow strangers to view images.

Other possible answers include:

- the sites might share location information via status updates
- they might give away personal information such as date of birth.

Control who has access

You can control who is able to access your personal spaces in the following ways:

- Make online albums **private**. You usually do this by entering the email addresses of those people you want to have access.
- **Don't befriend everyone** who sends a friend request on social networking sites. Check them out first.
- Check and use your **privacy settings** on all social networking sites.
- **Think** before you share anything online.

Five rules

1. Don't post anything online that you would not want made public.
2. Minimise details that identify you or your whereabouts.
3. Keep your account numbers, usernames and passwords secret.
4. Only share your screen names with people you know.
5. Don't use apps that use the GPS function on your phone to share your location with people you don't know.

Your online reputation

To find out what others have said:

- type your first and last name into several popular search engines
- search blogs and social networks to review what others have posted about you in comments, photos or videos.

If you find information about yourself that you are not happy about, act quickly. Ask the person who posted it to remove or correct the information, or ask the website administrator to remove offending material.

Now try this

Explain the privacy concerns associated with social networks.　**(3 marks)**

Information misuse

You need to know about **overt** and **covert** ways of collecting information.

To open an online account...

You have to submit personal information:

Title:	▼
Name:	
D.O.B:	
Address:	
Email:	

Reputable companies will keep your data secure and won't share it with other companies. They will ask you to 'opt in' to marketing emails rather than to 'opt out'.

To pay online...

You have to submit financial information:

Card Type:	▼
Name on Card:	
Card Number:	
Expiry Date:	
CCV:	

You should always check that the site is secure before you submit the information. Check for:

- **https** at the beginning of the address
- a **padlock**.

> You know that this information is being collected – it is **overt** data collection.

Worked example

target C-B

State what a cookie is and what it does. **(2 marks)**

Cookies are small text files sent to your computer by most websites when you visit them. They are stored on your computer and are used to track what you do on that website.

Companies use **cookies** to monitor what you look at and buy so they can suggest things you might like. Some sites allow **third party cookies** from marketing companies. They sell the information they find out about you.

Spyware

Hackers can install software called **Trojans** to spy on your computer.

- Trojans record all of your key strokes or take pictures of the screen.
- Hackers can find out your personal and financial information as you enter it, and use it to commit fraud.

> You don't know that this information is being collected – it is **covert** data collection.

Identity theft

If fraudsters find out people's personal details they can use them to make money by pretending to be that person. They can open bank accounts and apply for loans, credit cards, passports and driving licences, all in someone else's name.

Valuable information!

Organisations make money by selling personal information. For example, the government sells the personal details you give to tax your car through the DVLA to private companies.

Now try this

target C

(a) Give **one** benefit to you of a cookie. **(1 mark)**

target D-C

(b) Give **two** reasons why you should consider deleting cookies from your computer. **(2 marks)**

Preventing misuse

You need to be able to explain the precautions you should take to prevent the misuse of your personal information.

1 Controlling cookies

Cookies track your browsing activity and are a **major privacy concern**. All recent versions of popular browsers allow users to control cookies by:

- setting their browsers to accept or reject all or some cookies
- setting their browser to prompt them each time a cookie is offered.

All browsers also have an option to delete all of the cookies on your computer.

Privacy policies

Any website that collects information from its customers should have a privacy policy describing the website's use of cookies and other trackers.

Worked example

target C-B

edexcel

Companies publish privacy policies on their websites. Explain the purpose of a privacy policy.
(2 marks)

Reputable firms will have their privacy policy in a prominent place in line with the Data Protection Act. It will tell you what information will be gathered and how it will be stored and used.

EXAM ALERT!

Well over 9 out of 10 students failed to get both marks for this question. Students didn't understand that websites have a responsibility to keep data secure and let users know how it will be used.

This was a real exam question that a lot of students struggled with – **be prepared!**   ResultsPlus

2 Phishing: don't be fooled

Phishing emails are sent to get information out of people. Their tone is often urgent because they want you to hand over your information without thinking. The golden rule is that banks say they will never contact you by email asking for secure details. Phishing emails are becoming more sophisticated and the websites they send you to are hard to distinguish from the real ones. Look out for:

- **impersonal** greeting
- **threat**
- URL that appears to be from bank but doesn't take you to bank website when clicked
- **request for personal information.**

3 Preventing spyware

1. Use a firewall to prevent spyware being remotely downloaded to your computer.
2. Install antispyware protection software.
3. Be wary of downloading popular 'free' music and movie file-sharing programs.
4. Surf and download more safely:
   - Only download programs from websites you trust.
   - Read all security warnings, licence agreements and privacy statements.
   - Never click 'Agree' or 'OK' to close the window of a website you're not sure about. Use the red ⊗.

Now try this

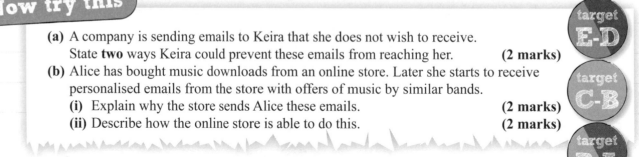

(a) A company is sending emails to Keira that she does not wish to receive. State **two** ways Keira could prevent these emails from reaching her.   **(2 marks)**   target E-D

(b) Alice has bought music downloads from an online store. Later she starts to receive personalised emails from the store with offers of music by similar bands.
   (i) Explain why the store sends Alice these emails.   **(2 marks)**   target C-B
   (ii) Describe how the online store is able to do this.   **(2 marks)**   target B-A

Legislation

The Data Protection Act and the Computer Misuse Act are designed to protect our privacy. You need to know about the legislation that safeguards your online privacy and security.

Data protection

It is easier to misuse data and information when it is stored online so it is important that data we submit online is kept secure. **The Data Protection Act 1998** was put in place to protect us. Companies holding our data are required by law:

- to keep it **secure**
- not to ask for **more data** than necessary
- not to keep data any **longer** than necessary
- to keep data **accurate** and up to date
- not to use data for any other purpose **without our consent**.

Worked example

Aisha likes to buy clothes online. The websites she uses hold her personal data. Describe the law that protects her data. **(2 marks)**

The Data Protection Act protects Aisha's personal data by ensuring that it is kept secure, accurate, up to date and private.

EXAM ALERT!

Students' knowledge of legislation is often poor. Be careful not to confuse questions like this with questions about security.

Students have struggled with exam questions similar to this – **be prepared!**

 ResultsPlus

Your data protection rights

1. You have the right to look at and check any personal data an organisation holds about you. The organisation can charge you to access this data.
2. You can demand that incorrect information is amended.
3. You can demand that the data is not used in any way that could harm or distress you.
4. You can demand that your data is not used for direct marketing.

The Computer Misuse Act 1990

With the widespread use of the Internet it is now easier to remotely log into a network or someone's computer to steal or corrupt data.

The Computer Misuse Act lists three levels of crime:

Unauthorised access to computer material	This includes logging into another person's computer with their password without their permission. It also includes stealing their documents and programs.
Unauthorised modification of computer material	This includes destroying or corrupting another user's files, modifying system files or the creation of a virus.
Unauthorised access to a computer with intent	This includes gaining access to financial or administrative records and using the information to commit a further crime, for example fraud.

Now try this

Many companies store customers' personal details.
Explain the rights of the customer with regards to this data. **(3 marks)**

Copyright

- The Copyright, Designs and Patents Act **protects people's original work** from being used without their permission.
- **All original work** is copyright, including everything that is freely available to download from the Internet. The person who creates a work owns the copyright and is the only person who has the right to reproduce, adapt or sell it.
- Copyright owners can use **Creative Commons licences** to allow certain uses of their work. For example they could choose to make an image free if used for educational purposes.

literature   music   art

films — **'original work'** — images

sound recordings   drama   software

Why bother with copyright?

- People spend a lot of time and money writing and recording these materials. They deserve to be paid for them.
- If professional artists cannot make any money from their work, then they will not be able to afford to create any more.

Consequences of illegal file sharing

- You can be prosecuted.
- Your Internet Service Provider may prevent you from using the Internet.
- If found guilty you could be sent to prison.
- It has a huge impact on the music and film industries.

These are all examples of copyright **infringement** (breaking copyright law):

- Sharing videos and music over the Internet.
- Copying and distributing copyright files, for example giving someone a copy of an album you've just bought.
- Pretending that someone else's work is your own, for example copying information and putting it in an essay or project.

Worked example

 edexcel

target **B-A**

Michael uses a search engine to choose an image to go on his blog.
Explain Michael's legal responsibilities when using images.   **(2 marks)**

Michael should not use the image without the permission of the copyright owner because he would be breaching copyright. He should ask the copyright owner's permission to use the image to protect intellectual property rights.

Now try this

target **C-B**

(a) Give **two** harmful effects to the music industry of the illegal copying and sharing of files.   **(2 marks)**

target **F**

(b) Toby asks Freddie to copy a game for him. State why Freddie should not do this.   **(1 mark)**

Online shopping 1

Online shopping refers to the buying and selling of goods and services using websites accessed through the Internet. You can buy both **physical goods**, for example books, and **non-physical goods**, for example music downloads. Some companies sell only online and some have 'real' shops as well.

Online shops

How do they work?

- Website displays the goods for sale.
- Customer places products in the virtual 'shopping basket'.
- Customer selects 'check out'.
- Payment is made and confirmed.
- Goods and services are despatched and delivered to customer.

Features

- Facility to sort and search for goods.
- Images provided of products.
- 24/7 availability.
- Comparison of prices to similar products.
- Recommendations for future purchases.
- Customer reviews of products.
- Some sites offer 'comparison sites'.
- Bookable delivery service, for example for food.

Online booking systems for travel, leisure and entertainment

How do they work?

- Booking system displays events available.
- Customer selects the seat/flight/holiday and places it in the virtual 'shopping basket'.
- Customer enters personal details.
- Payment is made and confirmed.
- Confirmation email ticket sent and customers print the 'ticket'.

Worked example

target **D-C**

State **two** features of an online booking system:

1 Facility to sort and search for seats and availability.
2 Customer reviews.

Other possible answers include:
- Compare prices from different sources.
- Immediate confirmation of your booking.
- Last minute offers.

Some services are only available for purchase online, for example London 2012 tickets.

Now try this

target **D-C**

State **two** features of an online shop that would be useful to people wanting to buy books. **(2 marks)**

Online shopping 2

You need to be able to describe the advantages and disadvantages of shopping **online** rather than on the **high street**.

Advantages and disadvantages for the customer

👍 Far greater choice because you are not limited to one geographical area.

👍 You can shop all day, every day.

👍 You can find the best price using price comparison websites.

👍 You do not have to leave the house.

👍 You have the right to return the goods for any reason within 7 days of delivery unless goods are customised.

👍 You can read other users' reviews of a product.

👎 You need Internet access and computer skills.

👎 You cannot pay using cash.

👎 You cannot see or touch products or try on clothes.

👎 You usually have to pay for delivery.

👎 You need to submit personal information through a website.

👎 There is a risk of not receiving goods or having personal details stolen on fraudulent websites.

Worked example

edexcel

target **F-E**

Gia wants to buy a new pair of shoes. She decides to shop online.

Give **two** advantages of shopping online for shoes rather than buying from a shop.

(2 marks)

1 She can buy them at any time of day or night.

2 There are more choices of shoes and of price.

EXAM ALERT!

You need to make sure your answers are relevant to buying shoes.

You could **not** say that it is **cheaper** or **faster** to shop online. Sometimes shops are cheaper than buying online, and online goods have to be delivered, which takes time.

This was a real exam question that a lot of students struggled with - **be prepared!**

Results **Plus**

Impact on businesses

Online businesses can be located anywhere, so they do not have to pay expensive high street **rental prices**. They also often need a **smaller staff**, which saves money. Because online businesses do not physically display their stock they can usually carry a **greater range** of products. They can also attract customers from **all over the world**.

Easier access for people with physical disabilities or young children

More choice for people in remote areas

Impact on lifestyles

Available any time for people who work unsocial hours

Reduced carbon footprint

Now try this

target **E-D**

Catherine has decided to buy a new coat. Give **two** disadvantages to Catherine of shopping online for the coat rather than buying it from a shop.

(2 marks)

Online auctions

Online auctions are very similar to traditional auctions, but buyers and sellers can be all over the world. This makes them popular because it is much easier and less time consuming to find the item or buyer that you need.

How do online auctions work?

| Seller and bidder create online accounts | → | Seller supplies a description and photograph of an item for auction | → | The bidder with the highest bid at a scheduled time 'wins' the item | → | The bidder is obliged to buy the item they have 'won' in the auction | → | The seller and bidder exchange emails to arrange payment and delivery |

Features of online auctions

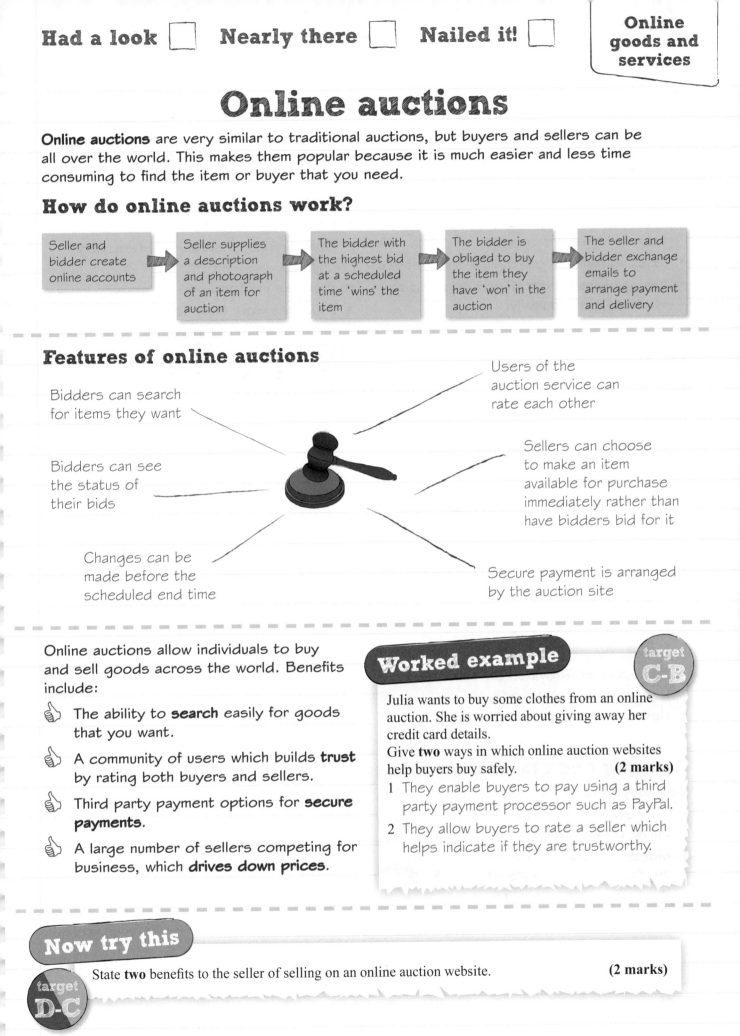

Bidders can search for items they want

Bidders can see the status of their bids

Changes can be made before the scheduled end time

Users of the auction service can rate each other

Sellers can choose to make an item available for purchase immediately rather than have bidders bid for it

Secure payment is arranged by the auction site

Online auctions allow individuals to buy and sell goods across the world. Benefits include:

👍 The ability to **search** easily for goods that you want.

👍 A community of users which builds **trust** by rating both buyers and sellers.

👍 Third party payment options for **secure payments**.

👍 A large number of sellers competing for business, which **drives down prices**.

Worked example

target C-B

Julia wants to buy some clothes from an online auction. She is worried about giving away her credit card details.
Give **two** ways in which online auction websites help buyers buy safely. **(2 marks)**

1 They enable buyers to pay using a third party payment processor such as PayPal.

2 They allow buyers to rate a seller which helps indicate if they are trustworthy.

Now try this

target D-C

State **two** benefits to the seller of selling on an online auction website. **(2 marks)**

Online education, news and banking

You need to understand how online services are provided for education, news and banking.

Education and training

How it works

- Student creates online account and selects his or her courses.
- Teaching material is provided on a website.
- Assignments submitted and returned to students electronically.

Features

- Interactive teaching material.
- Communities of students interacting online.
- Provides personalised learning.
- Students work from home.

Information services

How they work

- News reports are written by newspaper and TV companies. They are made available online for free or through a subscription.
- Users access the websites to read the news or select news using **RSS feeds**.

Features

- Easy to search for and sort news items.
- Up to date news available worldwide.
- Review news items from different sources.
- Allow users to select news.
- News presented in text, images and videos.
- Extra content provided for subscribers.
- Users can add comments.
- Users can subscribe to content.

Worked example

Give **two** drawbacks of accessing news and information online.   **(2 marks)**

1 Content presented as news but which is not from a reputable source may be biased or untrue.

2 People who do not have access to computers may miss important stories.

EXAM ALERT!

A similar question asked students to discuss online news services. Many students failed to give examples of the negative impacts. Make sure you know about the drawbacks, as well as the benefits, of online services.

Students have struggled with exam questions similar to this – **be prepared!**   ResultsPlus

Banking and other financial services

How they work

- User creates a secure online bank account.
- Money can be transferred electronically into account.
- Payments can be made to other accounts.

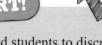

Features

- View up-to-date bank account details.
- View all transactions.
- Pay bills online.
- Create new bank accounts.
- Secure access provided.
- Offers promotions to online customers.

Now try this

target E-C

Heather works long hours. Give **two** advantages to Heather of an online banking system over telephone banking.   **(2 marks)**

Remember to make sure that you only give advantages that apply to online banking and **not** to telephone banking

Online gaming and entertainment

Online gaming enables players to connect via the Internet and interact with each other. 'On-demand' or **streaming** entertainment services allow users to play media when and where they want it.

Online gaming

A **central server** runs the game software and streams each player's position and actions **to all players** over the Internet.

Players need a **high bandwidth low latency** Internet connection to **avoid lag** when gaming.

Players **select game** and create **online accounts**, then **interact with each other** as well as a computer opponent.

Some games **store data** such as graphics and sound **locally** on players' computers.

Streaming versus downloading

Streaming, e.g. iPlayer

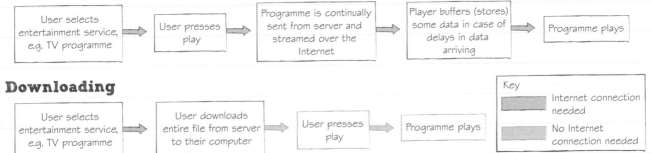

User selects entertainment service, e.g. TV programme → User presses play → Programme is continually sent from server and streamed over the Internet → Player buffers (stores) some data in case of delays in data arriving → Programme plays

Downloading

User selects entertainment service, e.g. TV programme → User downloads entire file from server to their computer → User presses play → Programme plays

Key
☐ Internet connection needed
☐ No Internet connection needed

Worked example

target
C-B

Shona uses an on-demand entertainment service to search for and watch TV programmes she has missed.
Give **two** other benefits to Shona of an on-demand entertainment service. **(2 marks)**

1 Do not have to wait for media to download before playing.

2 Does not use as much local storage.

A high bandwidth and low latency Internet connection improves the performance of streaming content.

Now try this

target
C-B

Sarah has just started gaming online.

(a) She creates an online account. Explain **one** benefit to Sarah of doing this. **(2 marks)**

target
B

(b) Describe how the actions of Sarah's character are communicated to other players. **(2 marks)**

(c) Sometimes Sarah experiences 'lag' in her games. Give **one** possible reason for this. **(1 mark)**

target
C

How and why organisations operate online

A website or online shop is the way in which organisations operate online. To operate successfully online, organisations need a website through which customers can find information and buy the organisation's goods and services. There are benefits to the organisation as well as to the customer.

Overheads (for example rent, salaries and fuel bills) are generally lower for online shops, so they can be **more profitable** than high street shops.

This means that online shops can afford to sell products more cheaply and still make a good profit.

> Questions that ask for three points rather than one are more difficult, but being able to answer them will help you to work at higher levels!

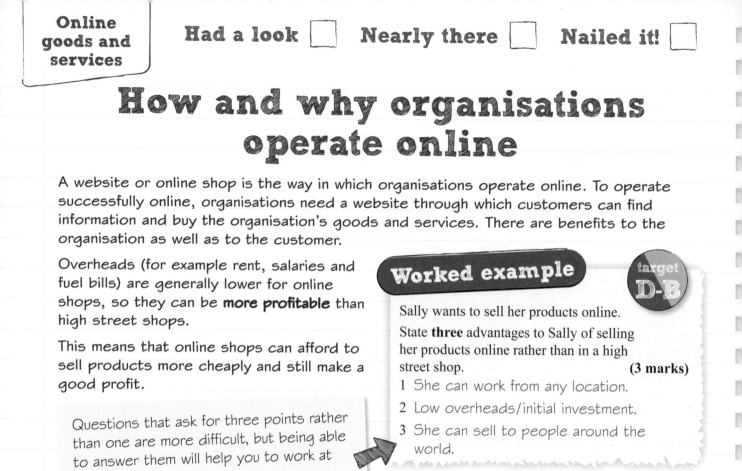

Worked example

target D-B

Sally wants to sell her products online.

State **three** advantages to Sally of selling her products online rather than in a high street shop.   **(3 marks)**

1 She can work from any location.

2 Low overheads/initial investment.

3 She can sell to people around the world.

Advantages and disadvantages for the retailer

👍 No need to distribute goods to shops.

👍 Easy to make changes to products and prices.

👍 Customers only need a web browser, an Internet connection and a means of paying electronically.

👍 Inexpensive way to reach new markets.

👍 Minimal start up time and investment needed: Internet businesses can be set up from home.

👍 The organisation can be located wherever it likes.

👎 Skilled staff needed to develop and run an efficient website.

👎 Ensuring online payment security is difficult.

👎 Need a delivery service and the facilities to handle returns.

👎 Customers limited to those with access to the Internet and who can pay electronically.

👎 If the retailer has high street shops as well, they may find that their high street shops suffer and have to close down because they cannot compete with the online shop.

Now try this

target D-A

PetzRUs is a high street pet shop. The owners are thinking of operating online.
Describe **two** advantages to PetzRUs of operating online as well as on the high street.   **(4 marks)**

Transactional data

Every time you buy something, online data about that **transaction** is saved. You need to know what transactional data is collected, how it is collected and what it is used for.

What is a transaction?

A transaction occurs every time you buy or sell something.

Transactional data is the information collected about that sale or purchase.

 This transactional data is stored in databases which can then be searched and sorted.

Personalised information is often stored in **cookies** (small text files) created on your computer when you visit a website.

Commercial value of transactional data

Transactional data is extremely valuable to the organisations you buy from because:

👍 it allows the organisation to keep a record of your purchases

👍 it allows delivery to be tracked

👍 it contains a rich source of information about customer shopping habits and preferences.

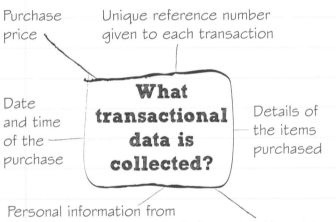

Purchase price

Unique reference number given to each transaction

What transactional data is collected?

Date and time of the purchase

Details of the items purchased

Personal information from your online account

Delivery tracking data that displays delivery status and location

What is transactional data used for?

- To understand customers' buying habits and to see trends in sales.
- To produce a more **personalised experience** (for example by showing other goods that you might be interested in).
- For **targeted advertising campaigns** and to produce **personalised adverts**.
- To create **personalised marketing** such as coupons for products that customers are likely to purchase.
- To track delivery of the goods.

Worked example

edexcel

target C-B

Laura receives an email with personalised offers on music similar to purchases she has made previously.
(a) Explain why the online store sends Laura the emails.
(2 marks)

Because the offers are relevant to previous purchases she may be persuaded to buy more.

target A-A*

(b) Describe how the online store is able to do this.   **(2 marks)**
The store has tracked data from previous transactions in her account or through cookies and has stored it in a database. They have queried the database and sent her an email about similar products.

Now try this

Give **two** ways in which companies use transactional data.   **(2 marks)**

target C-B

Had a look ☐ Nearly there ☐ Nailed it! ☐

Internet advertising 1

Internet advertising is another way in which organisations operate online. **Internet advertising** normally takes the form of text, image and videos including a link to the website where customers can buy goods or services.

Why do organisations use Internet advertising?

👍 It can be **targeted** at particular customers.

👍 Statistics can be **gathered**.

👍 It is **cheaper** than traditional advertising, for example TV adverts.

👍 It reaches a **wide range** of customers.

👍 It reaches customers much **faster** than traditional advertising.

Worked example

target D-A*

Mel sees some Internet advertisements. State **two** ways of advertising on the Internet. **(2 marks)**

1 Using search engines.
2 Using social networking sites.

Internet advertising using search engines

Advertisement is displayed when customers search using key words.

With Google Adwords the advertising company only pays Google when people click on their adverts. This is called 'cost-per-click'.

The key words have to be carefully chosen and the advert carefully worded to make people want to click on it.

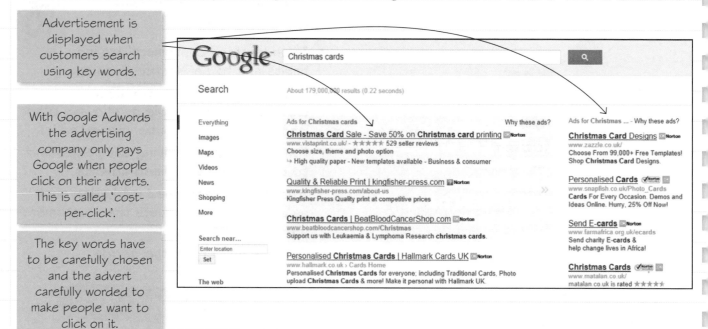

Internet advertising using social networking

- Many social networking sites use the information they know about users to **target** adverts at **particular users**.

- Organisations pay Facebook to display adverts on particular users' pages.

- Facebook, with more than 800 million users, can **select customers by location, age and interests**.

Now try this

target G-F

(a) Give **two** reasons why a company might want to advertise on the Internet. **(2 marks)**

(b) Give **two** drawbacks to a company of advertising on the Internet. **(2 marks)**

target E-D

Internet advertising 2

Viral marketing, targeted marketing and personalisation techniques (see page 48) are all about advertising goods and services online and trying to get customers to buy them.

Viral marketing

Viral marketing is when an organisation creates interesting and entertaining content that makes people want to 'pass it on' to their friends using social networking, email and texting.

Why is viral marketing used?

- If the content 'goes viral' it 'spreads' very quickly.
- It is cheap because the organisation does not have to pay for adverts.
- Memorable content means that people remember the brand name.

Start

Interesting and entertaining content, often video, is created that people will want to share. → The content is 'spread' by people sharing the content with their friends. → This is like the spread of a 'virus' between people.

Targeted marketing

Online targeted marketing is about concentrating online advertising on the groups of customers who are most likely to buy a product.

How does it work?

Online organisations collect and combine online data from:

- cookies that are used to store your browsing habits

- transactional data
- social networking sites
- microblogging sites
- personal information from online profiles.

The organisations then query that data to send adverts just to those users whose age, gender, interests or previous purchases suggest they might buy a particular product.

Now try this

Build'n'Fix uses online targeted marketing as part of its advertising campaign.

(a) Give **two** ways in which *Build'n'Fix* could obtain personal data from potential buyers. **(2 marks)**

(b) *Build'n'Fix* creates a viral advertisement. Give **one benefit** and **one drawback** of viral advertising for *Build'n'Fix*. **(2 marks)**

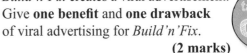

Internet advertising 3

Personalisation techniques

Personalisation techniques are used in targeted marketing. They make advertisements relevant to a particular customer using their personal information and have the aim of persuading the customer to buy related products.

For example, personalised emails, such as special occasion reminders, may be sent to your email address.

---

https://mail..com/mail

File   Edit   View   Favourites   Tools   Help

re: Your recent purchase - john@smith.net...

My email ✉

COMPOSE

Inbox
Sent items
Drafts
Spam
Deleted items

Dear Mr Smith,

Thank you for your recent purchase. We hope you are pleased with it. We thought you might be interested in these products based on your previous purchases.

More items to consider

Related to items you've viewed

Items you might like

> Adverts personalised using your past browsing and searching on other websites.

> Alternative products and favourite categories.

> Recommendations based on your browsing history and other items you may have purchased.

To **avoid** targeted marketing you can:

- opt out of sharing your personal information with other organisations when creating online accounts
- delete cookies
- be careful with the personal information you add to online profiles.

Worked example

target D-A

A company uses personalisation techniques as part of its online marketing. Give **one advantage** and **two disadvantages** to the **customer** of personalisation techniques. **(3 marks)**

Advantage: Customers are told about special offers that they are interested in, rather than just receiving general emails.

Disadvantage 1: The customer might find them annoying.

Disadvantage 2: Customers are only told about a limited range of products.

Another possible disadvantage is that personalisation techniques might stop customers coming across 'chance' items or items different from those they usually purchase.

Now try this

target B-A*

Describe **two** ways in which a company could use personalisation techniques to persuade people to buy their products. **(4 marks)**

Payment systems 1

Buying and selling online needs a secure payment system. Having confidence when paying for things online is important for all savvy users.

There are four ways of paying online:

1. credit/debit cards

2. online bank transfer (see page 50)

3. third party payment processors (see page 50)

4. online coupons and online gift vouchers/ eVouchers (see page 50).

Credit/debit cards

When you pay with a credit/debit card you are authorising the organisation you are buying from to transfer money from your bank account to its own bank account.

- **Debit cards** let the customer pay by taking money directly out of their account.

- **Credit cards** allow the customer to borrow the money. The customer pays the money back at a later date, often with interest.

When you pay online you give the following details:

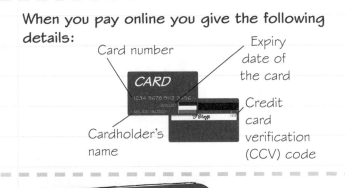

Card number — Expiry date of the card

CARD
1234 5678 9112 3456

Credit card verification (CCV) code

Cardholder's name

The Credit Card Verification (CCV) code is the number on the **back** of the card which is not included on the magnetic stripe or chip. Entering the CCV means the person entering the code must have seen the credit card.

Worked example

target **F**

Almut is nervous about shopping online. State the risk of using credit or debit cards for online purchases and describe one security method that websites can use to protect users.

Risk: The risk is that the details can be 'seen' as they are sent over the Internet.

Security method: To protect against this, online payment sites use the Secure Sockets Layer (SSL) which means data is encrypted to provide a secure transfer over the Internet. This means that the website has been investigated and is rated as trustworthy.

To make sure that a website is secure, look out for:

The URL changing from http to https

A change in the address bar's colour (often green)

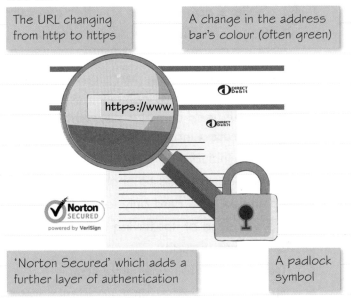

https://www.

'Norton Secured' which adds a further layer of authentication

A padlock symbol

Now try this

Sally is buying clothes from an online auction.
(a) Give **two** ways she could pay.
(2 marks)

(b) Give **two** things she should look out for to show that the website is secure.
(2 marks)

target **G-F**

target **E-C**

Payment systems 2

Other than credit/debit card, there are three more ways of making online payments.

Online bank transfer

Customers can make online payments directly from their account to other accounts as long as they know the bank account details of the organisation they are paying.

Online banks keep customers **safe from online fraud** by:

- checking bank accounts to make sure there is no unusual activity
- providing secure encrypted web services
- using login protection schemes such as PINsentry.

Online coupons and eVouchers

Many online shops now offer 'online' gift **eVouchers** or 'money off' coupons. These can be sent to people electronically by email, or printed out and sent by post.

To redeem the gift eVoucher or coupon the recipient creates an online account and enters the unique reference numbers given on the eVoucher or coupon.

Third party payment processors

Third party payment processors are trusted organisations who stand between the customers and the retailers so payments are **not made directly**.

PAYMENT Buyer's bank ⇒ Third party payment processor e.g. PayPal ⇒ Seller's bank

TRANSFER OF GOODS Buyer ⇐ Seller

1 The buyer creates a third party payment processor account which includes details of their credit/debit card. This information is never shared with retailers.

2 The buyer pays the third party who holds the money until payment is authorised.

3 Once payment has been authorised, the third party transfers it to the seller.

Advantages

👍 Sellers do not need to offer a secure site (which can be expensive).

👍 Buyers are not exposed to fraud.

Near field communication (NFC) is a **contactless payment service** which allows devices to **communicate** when **close together**. NFC **cards** can be used to **make payments**. NFC technology is now being **integrated** into mobile phones too.

Advantages include:

👍 Good security due to short transmission range.

👍 Losing an NFC card only loses the credit in the account.

👍 Convenience of not having to enter payment details repeatedly.

Disadvantages include:

👎 Can only pay for small amounts.

👎 Need to protect against accidental payments.

👎 If the NFC card is lost, anyone can use the credit on it.

Worked example

Emma is paying a bill online. She does not want to pay by credit or debit card.

State **three other** ways of making payments online.

(3 marks)

Third party payment processor, eVoucher or direct transfer from an online bank account

Now try this

Jackie is sent an eVoucher as a present.
Describe how she can use her eVoucher.

(2 marks)

Consumer protection

Consumer protection is about the laws that protect the rights of people who are buying things.

Consumer rights under UK Law

When you buy something, that item must be of satisfactory quality, fit for purpose and as described.

If the item is faulty it has to be replaced, repaired or the money refunded.

Shopping online

If you buy online from a UK-based retailer then you have the **same rights** buying online as you do buying in a shop. This means you can return faulty items just like you would in a shop.

Cooling off period

In addition to your normal rights, there is a **'cooling off' period** for online purchases. This means that orders placed online can be cancelled, for **any reason**, up to seven working days after receiving the items and a full refund of any money paid will be made.

This cooling off period applies to everything **except**:

- goods made to a personalised specification
- perishable goods, such as food and flowers
- CDs/DVDs/software where the seal has been broken
- newspapers, magazines or other reading material (not books)
- gaming, betting and lotteries.

Worked example   edexcel

target **E-B**

Stevie buys some clothes online.
She finds that the T-shirts do not match the description on the website.
Describe her consumer rights. **(2 marks)**

She is entitled to a refund as the product was not as it was described on the website. As long as she is buying from a UK-based retailer, she has the same rights under UK law as if she bought them in a shop.

EXAM ALERT!

Only one fifth of students gained full marks for this question. Many stated that she could get a refund but failed to say why in order to gain the second mark.

This was a real exam question that a lot of students struggled with – **be prepared!** ResultsPlus

Now try this

target **C**

Sarah buys a new dress from an online shop based in the UK. When it arrives she finds that it is too small.
State why she has the right to return it. **(1 mark)**

Applications software

Applications software is software used to carry out a particular task e.g. a game or a word processor. There are two types of application software.

1 Locally installed software

User obtains software on DVD or downloads from Internet ➡ User installs software on computer or file server

Advantages
👍 Works without being online.
👍 You hold the licence to use the software.
👍 You control access to the computer so security is good.

Disadvantages
👎 Takes up a large amount of file space.
👎 Must download and install upgrades and patches to fix bugs.
👎 All data is stored locally so it must be backed up.

2 Hosted software (Software as a Service)

User logs in through Internet to use software when needed ➡ Software runs on a web server over the Internet

Advantages
👍 Software doesn't take up any file space on your computer.
👍 Allows users from different parts of the world to work on the same document at the same time.

Disadvantages
👎 Cannot work without an Internet connection.
👎 Not as secure – hosting company might be targeted by online hackers.
👎 Response time depends on network speed.

Proprietary or open source?

Proprietary software is developed by a company. You usually have to **pay** to use it on your computer or online.

Microsoft Word is proprietary software

Open source software is developed by volunteers who gradually improve it. It is **free** to use on your computer or online.

OpenOffice.org is open source software

Worked example   edexcel

target E-C

Lee recommends that open source software is installed on some laptops.

(a) Give **two** advantages of open source software over proprietary software. **(2 marks)**
1 Free.
2 You can modify the software to make it more suitable for your needs.

(b) Give **one** disadvantage of open source software over proprietary software. **(1 mark)**
Doesn't always have the same features as proprietary software.

Other disadvantages of open source software:
• No technical help.
• No guarantee that bugs will be fixed.
• Fewer security features than proprietary.

Now try this

Describe the difference between locally installed software and hosted software. **(2 marks)**

target F-E

Commercial response to SaaS

Hosted software or **'software as a service'** (SaaS) is when you run applications (such as a word processor or spreadsheet) in a **web browser**. The applications are not installed on your local computer.

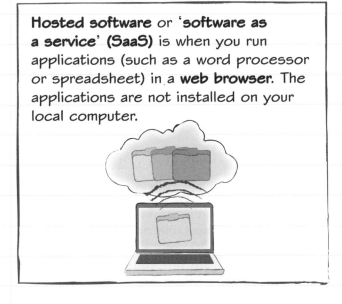

Commercial software producers such as Microsoft make money by selling software applications such as word processors (Word) and spreadsheets (Excel).

Some 'software as a service' applications are now available for free, for example GoogleDocs, so the business of commercial providers could be **threatened** as customers use the free 'software as a service' online applications.

Commercial software producers have had to come up with ways to ensure that customers are still willing to pay for their software.

Responses to SaaS

To **respond** to this challenge the commercial software producers have:

- Made their products more appealing and of better quality by including more facilities and functions.

- Provided software 'bundled' in when you buy a computer. So when you buy a PC or laptop it often comes with software applications installed.

- Provided technical support, help services and training materials.

- Used copyright to protect their products to stop similar 'free' products being offered as a 'software service'.

- Offered their own versions of software as a service.

Worked example

Give **one** benefit to the environment of hosted software.   **(1 mark)**

Every year millions of boxes of software and millions of music CDs go to landfills. Software as a service is delivered without packaging or CDs, so helps reduce this.

Make sure you read the question carefully. In the exam, it would be easy to give a benefit to the user of hosted software, rather than a benefit to the environment, which is what the question asks for.

Now try this

Some commercial software producers respond to free software as a service by pre-installing their software on new computers.

Give **one** other way in which commercial software producers can respond to free software as a service.   **(1 mark)**

Remember: 'software as a service' is when we use software applications over the Internet using a web browser rather than programs installed on our computer.

Storage: local or online?

Data storage refers to the data you store in files. They can be documents, pictures, spreadsheets, videos or music files.

Local data storage is when your files are stored on the digital device you are using.

Online data storage is when your files are stored on a server elsewhere which you access using the Internet. This is referred to as 'in the cloud'.

---

1 Local storage

👍 You have control over access to your files and the security of the data.

👍 Data can be accessed quickly.

👍 You do not need an Internet connection to access the data.

👎 You are responsible for keeping the data safe.

👎 It is difficult to share your data with others.

👎 You have to back up your data.

2 Online storage

👍 The data is available anywhere you have Internet access and a browser.

👍 Some online data storage services are free.

👍 It is easy to share your data with others.

👍 Data is backed up for you.

👎 You have to trust that the organisation storing your data will keep your data secure.

👎 The online data storage may not be reliable.

👎 You need an Internet connection to get access to your data. This can be frustrating if the connection is slow.

👎 Less control of your data as you do not know where your data is stored.

Worked example

target E-D

Pippa wants to store her video files securely. Give **two** advantages to Pippa of using online storage rather than DVD.

1 She can access her video files from anywhere with a browser and Internet connection.

2 She could lose or break a DVD, but this cannot happen with online storage.

Other possible answers include:
- regularly backed-up
- easier to share with others.

Now try this

target F-D

Seb stores his digital photos online. He can access them from anywhere he has Internet access. Give **two other** benefits to Seb of using online storage rather than local storage. **(2 marks)**

Search engines

It is important that you understand how to use search engines **effectively**.

A search engine is a computer program that searches for web content that contains, or is tagged with, the **key words** you have entered into the search box.

The search engine then searches its **indexes** for content containing those key words and displays a list of the content that is matched.

YAHOO! Google

Remember no one checks or verifies that websites contain truthful information.

Search techniques

Your choice of key words is important.

- Add more key words to narrow down the search.
- Search by the type of object you are searching, for example image, a web page, news, maps, or videos.
- Use the advanced search facilities of the search engine.
- Search by date/language.
- Use more than one search engine. Different search engines give different results.

Use different types of search to gain more specific results:

Search term	What it finds
'Snow White'	Finds the exact phrase
Snow AND White or Snow + White	Finds all web pages containing both Snow and White
Snow OR White	Finds web pages containing either Snow or White
Snow NOT white or Snow – White	Finds web pages which contain Snow but not White

Validity of search results

It is important that you check which search results are valid because some websites might infect your computer with spyware, contain biased or inappropriate content, or simply not be about exactly the subject you are after.

Other correct answers would be:
- He could look at the summary to see if the website contains relevant information.
- He could look at the summary to see if there are any spelling mistakes, or look at the preview to see if the website looks professional, or if it is full of adverts.

Worked example

Ted is researching information for a school project.
He searches the web for relevant information.
Give **two** ways in which Ted could check the reliability of the search results.   **(2 marks)**

1 He could look at the URLs to check that the results come from a trusted organisation.

2 He could check that the information is up to date.

Now try this

target
C-A

Describe **one** way in which users can refine web searches to improve the validity of results.   **(2 marks)**

Online communities – what are they?

An online community is a group of people who meet up online. You need to understand about different types of online communities, their features and their functions.

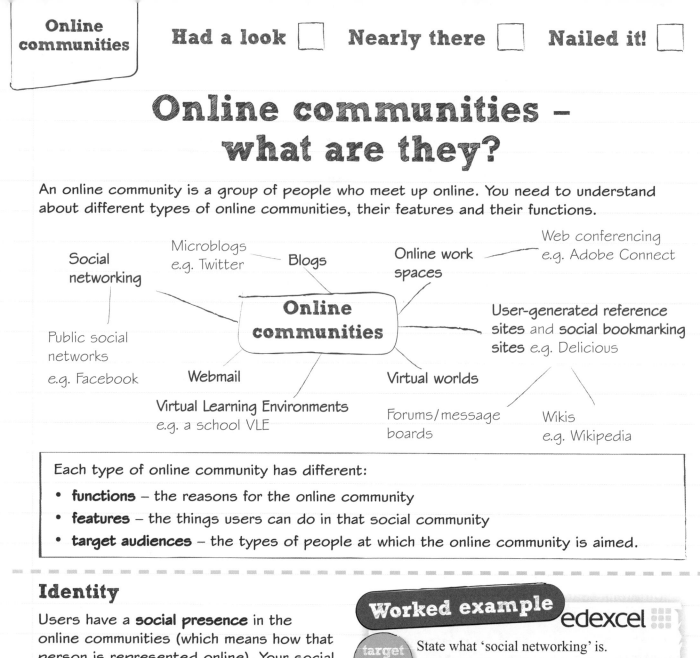

Social networking

Microblogs e.g. Twitter

Blogs

Online work spaces

Web conferencing e.g. Adobe Connect

Public social networks e.g. Facebook

Online communities

User-generated reference sites and **social bookmarking** sites e.g. Delicious

Webmail

Virtual worlds

Virtual Learning Environments e.g. a school VLE

Forums/message boards

Wikis e.g. Wikipedia

Each type of online community has different:

- **functions** – the reasons for the online community
- **features** – the things users can do in that social community
- **target audiences** – the types of people at which the online community is aimed.

Identity

Users have a **social presence** in the online communities (which means how that person is represented online). Your social presence is developed as you contribute online to the social community.

Most online communities require you to have an **online account** with a **username** and **password**. Changing your **user profile** allows you to create your online social presence.

EXAM ALERT!

Less than one in seven students got this right. Make sure you understand what terms mean as well as knowing examples of them.

This question was looking for students to mention the concept of 'connecting', or 'linking' to other users in some way.

This was a real exam question that a lot of students struggled with – **be prepared!** ResultsPlus

Now try this

target **E-D**

(a) List **two** types of online community.
(2 marks)

target **C-A**

(b) Give **two** reasons for having an online account in an online community. **(2 marks)**

Online workspaces and VLEs

Online workspaces provide an online community for a group of people who **work** together, whereas **Virtual Learning Environments (VLEs)** provide an online community for a group of people who **learn** together.

Online workspaces

Online workspaces provide a virtual space for people who work together to meet, share files and work collaboratively online.

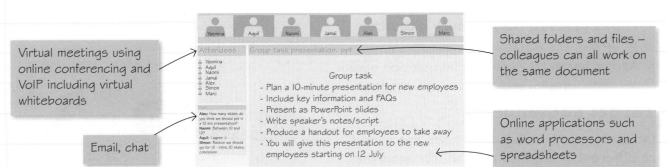

Virtual meetings using online conferencing and VoIP including virtual whiteboards

Email, chat

Shared folders and files – colleagues can all work on the same document

Online applications such as word processors and spreadsheets

Group task
- Plan a 10-minute presentation for new employees
- Include key information and FAQs
- Present as PowerPoint slides
- Write speaker's notes/script
- Produce a handout for employees to take away
- You will give this presentation to the new employees starting on 12 July

Virtual Learning Environments (VLEs)

Functions

- Provide information to help students learn, for example access to additional notes and homework in school or remotely from home as long as they have an Internet connection.

- Allow teachers to work collaboratively to create high quality learning material.

Features

- timetable/'news' for staff and students
- marking tools for the teachers
- email and chat communication
- students, teachers and parents can track progress and data such as test marks
- personalisation for individual students
- interactive polls and questionnaires
- facility for students to contribute to blogs and personalise their own space.

Worked example

edexcel

target C-B

Give **three** ways a team could use an online workspace to work collaboratively. **(3 marks)**

1 They can all work on the same document.
2 They can hold a virtual meeting using chat.
3 They can use VoIP.

EXAM ALERT!

Only one in four students achieved full marks on this question. Many gave examples of online communities instead. Make sure you read the question carefully.

This was a real exam question that a lot of students struggled with – **be prepared!**

ResultsPlus

Now try this

target D-B

Jake is producing a company newsletter with his French colleague, Céline, using an online workspace.

(a) Describe the function of an online workspace. **(2 marks)**

(b) The online workspace allows Jake to set access permissions on the files.

target A

Give **one other** advantage to Jake and Céline of using an online workspace rather than email. **(1 mark)**

Social networks

A **social networking site** is an online community where people are **linked** together using their **personal information**.

Functions

- Allow users to have an online presence.
- Links users with others using personal information.
- Allows users to stay in touch with other people.
- Allows users to exchange information such as photographs and videos with others.

Target audience

Different social networking sites are aimed at different groups of people. For example:

- **LinkedIn** is aimed at business people with advice given by industry experts.
- **Bebo** is aimed at younger teens with areas for gaming and music videos.

Worked example

target E-C

Give **two** advantages of using social networks, rather than SMS, to stay in touch with friends. **(2 marks)**

1 Only have to post one message to reach many people.

2 SMS requires payment for each person receiving the message.

EXAM ALERT!

In a very similar question, students often made the mistake of saying that social networking is free, when actually you must pay for your Internet access.

Students have struggled with exam questions similar to this – **be prepared!**   Results**Plus**

I interact with other people using chat and email, and by sharing photo and video files

I personalise my own space by adding photos and links, and by changing the layout

I earn 'credits' which I can use in games and to buy things

I share links to music sites, blogs and other websites that interest me

I play games

I can access the site from an app on my mobile phone

I can 'like' other users' content

Advantages and disadvantages of social networking

- 👍 Easy for everyone to create a personal page.
- 👍 Easy way to keep in contact with people.
- 👍 Easy to make new friends with similar interests.
- 👍 You can post interesting things about yourself.
- 👍 Often free to join and use.
- 👍 Easy way to share different types of information, for example video, and to organise pictures.
- 👍 Efficient way to communicate with a lot of people.
- 👍 Moderators help to prevent inappropriate posting.

- 👎 People can waste a lot of time.
- 👎 Some people create fake profiles.
- 👎 Loss of privacy.
- 👎 Online bullying.
- 👎 Posting content such as compromising photos may prove embarrassing.
- 👎 GPS tagging may be a risk to users' safety if their location is given away.
- 👎 Inexperienced users may give away personal details that risk their personal safety or security (for example identity theft).

Now try this

Sarah has just joined a new social network.

target D-C
(a) List **two** features of social networks. **(2 marks)**

target C-A
(b) Explain why different social networks have different features. **(3 marks)**

User-generated reference sites

User-generated reference sites, for example wikis, allow users to contribute and share information.

Functions

User-generated reference sites allow users to generate content collaboratively on a website. Different websites have different functions for example:

- **Wikis** are websites where users can add or edit content collaboratively using **wiki software**. One example is **Wikipedia**, which is a free, web-based encyclopaedia.
- **Internet forums** or **message boards** allow people to hold discussions by posting messages about a certain subject.
- **Newsgroups** are communities, like message boards, that allows users to discuss a particular topic.
- **Review sites** allow users to post reviews to inform potential customers of the product/service they are considering buying.

Target audience

The target audience is therefore anyone who wants to contribute to the site and to access the information stored on the site. Different websites will have different audiences.

Features

- Ability for all users to add and edit the content, for example text and images, in a wiki reference site such as Wikipedia using only a simple browser.
- Changes can be tracked to see who has made contributions.
- Hyperlinked pages and images.

The Wikipedia logo

Advantages and disadvantages of wikis

👍 Wikis can be easily changed by users so the information on the websites can be **up to date**.	👎 As anyone can contribute information, it can become **inaccurate, biased or untrue** if not carefully managed.
👍 People from **different parts of the world** can work together to create content.	👎 An **Internet connection** is needed for people to work collaboratively.
👍 They often do not require users to pay a fee and contain a **huge amount of information**.	👎 The information may become **disorganised** and include errors and duplication.

Henry is using information from a wiki to help him with his school project.
Explain **one** concern Henry may have when using information from a wiki.   **(2 marks)**
Anyone can add material to a wiki, so the information might be biased or inaccurate.

---

target **D-B**

Wikipedia is an example of a user-generated reference site.
List **three** features of a user-generated reference site.   **(3 marks)**

Social bookmarking sites

You will need to understand how social bookmarking websites differ from user-generated reference sites, as well as the features they offer.

Functions

Social bookmarking websites are similar to wikis, but users add bookmarks (weblinks) rather than content, then share these bookmarks with others.

One example is Pinterest where users create 'pinboards' to organise and share images they like on the web.

Digg is a social news website which allows people to share news and rate its importance.

Delicious allows users to create 'stacks' of content (videos, images, blogs, tweets and so on) on a particular theme.

Features

- Users can store URLs online.
- Users give tag words to categorise the URLs.
- The tags can then be used to search bookmarks by topic/category.
- Users can share their bookmarks with others online.
- Users can search for similar bookmarks from other users using tags.
- Users can like or dislike content.

Worked example

target B

Poppy is using a social bookmarking site to share images she is collecting as inspiration for her D&T project.
Give **two** features of a social bookmarking website that would be useful to Poppy. **(2 marks)**

1 URLs of images can be stored online so that she does not lose them.

2 URLs can be accessed from any device connected to the Internet.

Another possible answer is that she can share her ideas with friends and her teacher to gain feedback.

Now try this

target D-B

Describe **one** function of a social bookmarking site. **(2 marks)**

Creation of knowledge

You need to understand how ICT and online communities have changed the way in which knowledge is created.

How online communities have changed the way knowledge is created

Knowledge is the information and skills gained through experience or education.

Tools such as spreadsheets and databases help to create ideas, **model** different situations and **solve problems**

People can communicate, collaborate and share ideas on a **global scale**

Information is **constantly updated** and is always open for improvement, for example entries on Wikipedia

Information and knowledge can be made **accessible** to everyone through ICT. University students can take courses and communicate with their tutors online

Users, rather than editors, can decide what information is important, for example Digg users can 'bury' news that they deem unimportant or inappropriate

---

Over 500 years ago the invention of the printing press changed the lives of ordinary people because they could afford books and learn to read. In a similar way, the Internet has enabled ordinary people to publish their ideas and information online.

The ability to create content and knowledge and publish information is no longer confined to traditional publishers and newspapers, but is open to anyone with an Internet connection. This has made an enormous difference to the way we create and share information.

👍 A large number of viewpoints can give richer, more rounded picture.

👎 The variety of viewpoints can be **overwhelming** for users.

👎 In many cases, nobody checks or edits what is published online, so it is important to be able to **select** what is relevant to you and also to know which information comes from a **valid source**.

Worked example

target A–A*

Give **two** ways in which the Internet has improved users' interaction with news. **(2 marks)**

1 People can rate stories to promote or bury them.

2 Everyone can publish and comment on news stories.

Other possible answers include:
- Latest news can be added easily to a variety of websites through news feeds.
- Users, rather than editors, can decide what information is important.

Describe **two** ways in which ICT is changing the way knowledge is created. **(4 marks)**

61

Impact on working practices

You need to understand how ICT and online communities have changed the way in which people work.

👍 Many workers now **telecommute** and work from home. You no longer have to live close to where you work.

👍 **Cloud computing** allows workers to access documents and programs from anywhere they can get Internet access.

👍 **Decisions** can be made more effectively through an online workspace as everyone can see and agree changes to a document at the same time.

👍 Employers can check social networks to **research potential employees**.

👎 People may avoid **face-to-face contact**, for example emailing someone a few desks away.

👎 Some employees may feel **pressured** to work when away from the office.

👎 Workers without Internet access may be **left out** of making important decisions.

👎 Some employees have been disciplined for **defamatory posts** on social networks because such posting is considered to be the same thing as publishing in a newspaper.

Worked example

target C-B

Steve lives a long way from his office so works part-time from home.
List **two** ways in which technology can help him to access documents and people in the office. **(2 marks)**

1 He can access any of his documents remotely using cloud computing.

2 He can communicate effectively with colleagues using email, VoIP or collaborative online workspaces.

The Internet helps people to work in different ways:

Collaborative working is about working together as a group to achieve common goals. This can be helped by VoIP, email, online chat, social networking and online work spaces.

👍 Users can work together on the same documents online and share ideas 👍 Working as a group, users can get more work done in less time 👍 Users can help each other solve problems	👎 Cannot read body language in meetings 👎 Work can be lost if users overwrite others' contributions

Teleworking is about working at home but staying in touch with others with the help of technology.

👍 Saves money – no need to pay for transport to work 👍 Flexible – people can work when and where they like 👍 Increased productivity – less time lost travelling 👍 Reduces pollution – no need to travel to work	👎 Less social contact – can feel isolated 👎 It is easy to work for long hours and get no break 👎 Distractions at home so work does not get completed 👎 Dependent on having an Internet connection

---

Now try this

target E-C

List **two** ways in which the Internet helps people to work collaboratively. **(2 marks)**

Socialising and responsible use

Socialising is about how you get along with others. The Internet has created new ways of socialising, e.g.

- social networking, microblogging, online games, chat rooms, VoIP, emails and virtual worlds
- websites such as 'Friends Reunited' allow people to find and get in touch with old friends
- online dating is becoming more popular.

The Internet has had both good and bad impacts on socialising:

- 👍 Easy way for people to keep in contact.
- 👍 Easy translations between languages.
- 👍 Available 24/7/365.
- 👎 Need an Internet connection to keep in touch.
- 👎 People can pretend to be someone they're not.
- 👎 People spend less time with real friends.

Behaving in an acceptable way includes:

- respecting other people's computers and files
- keeping your passwords private
- keeping your computer safe by using antivirus software and firewalls
- respecting others' opinions online
- thanking people online
- abiding by copyright law by not making unauthorised copies of files
- not posting inappropriate images or videos.

Acceptable use policies

When you set up an online account you are asked to agree to the rules given in an **acceptable use policy** or **code of conduct**.

Breaking the rules will result in your online account being withdrawn.

ACCEPTABLE USE POLICY

ACCEPTABLE USE POLICY

- I will keep my username and password secure
- I won't use someone else's username and password
- I won't use strong or offensive language
- I won't take or distribute images of someone without their permission

☐ I have read and understood these rules

☐ I agree to follow these rules

Worked example

target C-B

(a) Describe the purpose of an acceptable use policy. **(3 marks)**

An acceptable use policy is a set of rules that set out how to behave when using the website. Users have to agree to the rules before using the website.

target F-D

(b) Give **two** reasons why websites have an acceptable use policy. **(2 marks)**

1 To protect users from abuse.
2 To protect users from inappropriate content.

EXAM ALERT!

Very few students answered a similar question well. It is important to understand policies and what they mean in practice.

Students have struggled with exam questions similar to this – **be prepared!**

ResultsPlus

Now try this

Clare socialises online.

(a) List **two** ways in which the Internet is used for socialising. **(2 marks)**

target G-F

(b) Another user sends Clare a threatening message.

Describe **one** action Clare could take as a result of this. **(2 marks)**

target F-D

A global scale

ICT and the Internet allow us all to communicate and collaborate on a global scale. **Globalisation** means the increasing global relationships between cultures, people and economic activity.

- ICT has speeded up the process of **globalisation**.
- It is now easy to make **purchases from around the world** 24/7/365, so different time zones and public holidays in different countries do not prevent sales being made.
- We can select and pay for goods from around the world **without leaving our homes**.
- Helped by ICT, many **companies have now 'gone global'** with offices and customers around the world.
- Some countries now **censor or control access** to social networking sites and search engines to help them control access to information. The reasons for this are often:
  - politics – to repress opposition to the government
  - security – to prevent dangerous plans, e.g. terrorism, being coordinated online
  - protection – to protect people, for example children, from harmful content.

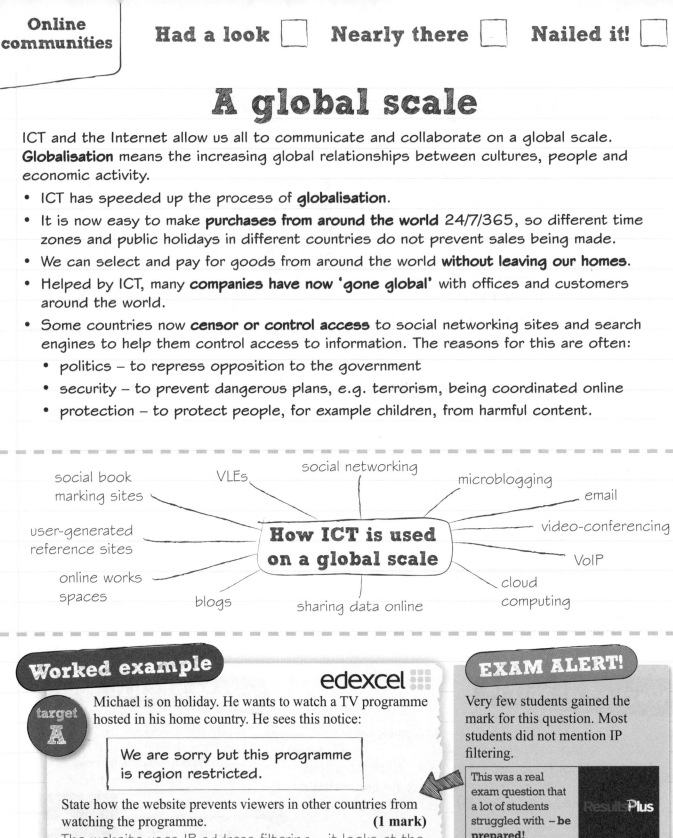

social book marking sites

VLEs

social networking

microblogging

email

user-generated reference sites

video-conferencing

How ICT is used on a global scale

VoIP

online works spaces

blogs

sharing data online

cloud computing

Worked example

edexcel ▦

target **A**

Michael is on holiday. He wants to watch a TV programme hosted in his home country. He sees this notice:

> We are sorry but this programme is region restricted.

State how the website prevents viewers in other countries from watching the programme. **(1 mark)**

The website uses IP address filtering – it looks at the IP address of the user to see which country they are in and does not allow users from other countries to access the programme.

EXAM ALERT!

Very few students gained the mark for this question. Most students did not mention IP filtering.

This was a real exam question that a lot of students struggled with – **be prepared!**

ResultsPlus

Now try this

target **C-B**

(a) Stella is a travel writer. Whilst abroad she uses an online workspace with colleagues in the UK.
List **two other** ways she could collaborate globally. **(2 marks)**

(b) Stella sometimes travels to places where there is no Wi-Fi connection. State **one other** type of wireless connectivity she could use to access the online workspace. **(1 mark)**

target **D**

Security issues

The next nine pages cover a range of **issues** you should be aware of in ICT. You may have revised them earlier in the guide because these issues arise in many areas of the specification. They are summarised here because it is important to understand them!

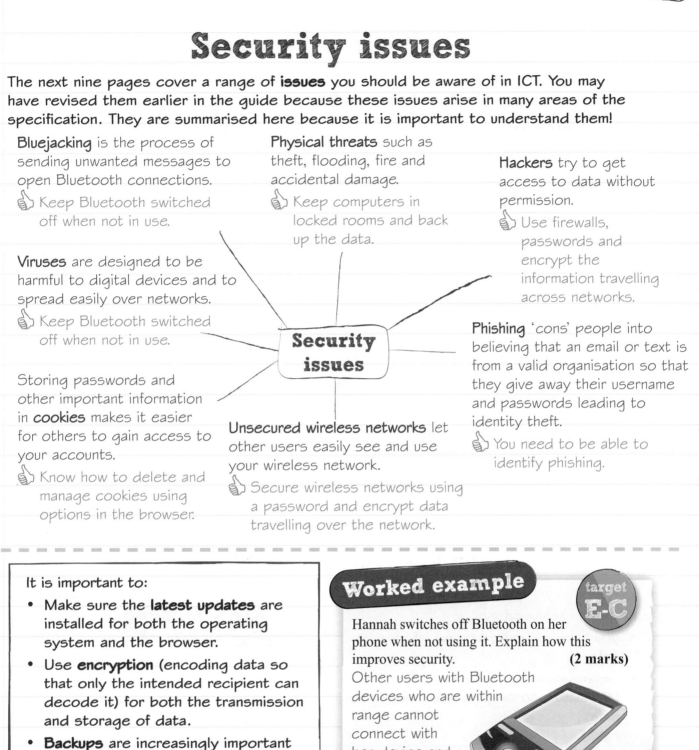

Bluejacking is the process of sending unwanted messages to open Bluetooth connections.

👍 Keep Bluetooth switched off when not in use.

Viruses are designed to be harmful to digital devices and to spread easily over networks.

👍 Keep Bluetooth switched off when not in use.

Storing passwords and other important information in **cookies** makes it easier for others to gain access to your accounts.

👍 Know how to delete and manage cookies using options in the browser.

Physical threats such as theft, flooding, fire and accidental damage.

👍 Keep computers in locked rooms and back up the data.

Security issues

Unsecured wireless networks let other users easily see and use your wireless network.

👍 Secure wireless networks using a password and encrypt data travelling over the network.

Hackers try to get access to data without permission.

👍 Use firewalls, passwords and encrypt the information travelling across networks.

Phishing 'cons' people into believing that an email or text is from a valid organisation so that they give away their username and passwords leading to identity theft.

👍 You need to be able to identify phishing.

It is important to:

- Make sure the **latest updates** are installed for both the operating system and the browser.

- Use **encryption** (encoding data so that only the intended recipient can decode it) for both the transmission and storage of data.

- **Backups** are increasingly important as threats to digital devices increase and as people live more and more of their lives online. The development of cloud computing allows users to back up their data remotely.

Hannah switches off Bluetooth on her phone when not using it. Explain how this improves security. **(2 marks)**

Other users with Bluetooth devices who are within range cannot connect with her device and send unwanted messages to her.

Now try this

target **D-C**

John is worried about data security. State **two** ways he can protect his data when using his smartphone. **(2 marks)**

Make sure your answers relate to methods of protecting data (which is what the question asks for). The response 'Turn off Bluetooth to prevent Bluejacking' would not gain a mark, as Bluejacking is not a threat to John's data.

Privacy issues

Privacy means keeping some personal aspects of your life private. Your privacy in the UK is protected legally by the **Data Protection Act**.

Social networking sites keep track of all your interactions and save them so they can be used later.

👍 Know how to use the privacy settings.

👍 Be aware of how much (and what type of) personal information you share online.

Search engines record information about your searches including your location (from your IP address), the time you spend searching and the searches you made, to help personalise your searches and display relevant online adverts. This information could make it easier for hackers to gain users' personal information and to steal their identity.

👍 Sign out of relevant accounts, especially on public computers.

People may post photographs online and add a **tag** to link names or other information with the photograph. This is considered an invasion of privacy.

👍 Educate friends about the risks and express your preferences to them.

You may be tricked into downloading **spyware**, allowing others to spy on the information on your computer.

👍 Use up-to-date antispyware software.

Threats to privacy

Hackers gain unauthorised access to your digital devices and access your personal information.

👍 Use firewalls, passwords and encrypt information sent across networks.

Identity theft involves someone pretending to be another person by collecting information about their identity.

👍 Keep all personal information safe.

Cookies are small text files stored on your computer and they can store your browsing habits and frequently visited websites. This can help with advertising relevant products, but may be seen as a privacy issue.

👍 Know how to delete and manage cookies.

Privacy is achieved by:

- you keeping your personal information safe

- organisations you give your personal information to keeping your information safe.

Worked example

An online shop stores customers' details on a computer. The computer is in a locked room and uses a firewall.
Explain **one other** way of preventing unauthorised users from reading the data in the database. **(2 marks)**

It could encrypt the data so that it could only be read by people with the encryption key.

 target B-A

Now try this

 target C-B

(a) Cookies can be seen as risks that make it easier for others to gain access to your accounts. But there are some benefits to the user as well.
Give **two benefits** of cookies to a user.
(2 marks)

(b) Some criminals steal personal information from Internet users. List **two** methods that criminals could use to collect personal information online. **(2 marks)**

target D-B

Monitoring movements and communications

You need to understand how ICT is being used to **monitor** how we move about and how we communicate.

When we travel abroad our **passports** are scanned and our movements in and out of different countries are monitored.

Geolocation information from GPS-enabled devices can track your position.

Mobile phone companies can track your movements as you move from base station to base station. Phone companies also know who we have been in phone/SMS contact with.

Playing **online games** means information about you and who you are playing with is being monitored.

Ways of monitoring people using ICT

Your computer's **IP address** provides clues to search engines and social networking sites about your geographical location.

Social networking sites store a rich source of information about our movements and communications. Geotagging from photographs posted online can be used to monitor your movements.

Companies providing **email services** know who you send emails to.

The use of **credit/debit cards** allows the banks to know when, where and how much money you spend.

Worked example

edexcel

Some social networking services use GPS data.
Explain how the irresponsible use of GPS data could place social network users at risk. **(2 marks)**

GPS data gives away the user's location. This could be dangerous if someone wanted to cause harm to that person, as they could go and find them.

EXAM ALERT!

Less than a third of students gained full marks for this question. Many gained one mark for saying that you could identify location from GPS data, but often failed to gain the second mark because they did not say why this was a risk.

This was a real exam question that a lot of students struggled with – **be prepared!**   ResultsPlus

For 'Explain' questions make sure you use your EEERs! (Expand by Explaining with Examples and Reasons)

Now try this

(a) State **two** ways people may use ICT to monitor your location. **(2 marks)**

(b) State **two** ways in which people may track your communications. **(2 marks)**

target E-C

target D-B

Health and safety

Using ICT can have both positive and negative effects on our physical health and mental well-being.

Positive effects

👍 Friendships can be built online using social networking.

👍 Easier to maintain contact with family and friends, especially those who live far away.

👍 Easier to access information, letting us learn new things.

👍 Exercises at home using games such as the Wii can improve physical fitness.

👍 Accurate health and fitness monitoring.

👍 ICT skills can help us get better paid and more skilled jobs.

👍 Mobile phones can help us keep safe by always being able to contact others.

👍 GPS technology can help us to find our location and guide us along routes.

Negative effects and ways to combat them

👎 ICT can contribute to obesity due to inactivity.

> Use of ICT should be balanced with other activities.

👎 People can always access their work, even on holiday or in the evening, so can become ill or stressed as they feel they are unable to stop working.

> People should maintain a 'work–life balance' by considering when they use ICT for work.

👎 Overuse of social networking sites and microblogging sites.

> Track time online, balance this with seeing family and friends in person.

👎 Repetitive strain injuries can develop from doing the same thing again and again.

> Change position or controller, and use supports.

👎 Joint pain can result from sitting incorrectly for a long time.

> Use an adjustable monitor and chair; do not sit for too long without a break.

👎 Eye strains can be caused by staring at a screen for a long time.

> Use a screen filter and take regular breaks.

👎 The radio waves from mobile phones and base stations may affect health.

> Use hands-free devices for longer calls.

👎 Accidents can be caused by people using mobile phones whilst driving.

> Always use hands-free devices when driving.

Worked example

target E-D

Repetitive strain injury (RSI) is associated with playing video games. State **two** ways Mark can prevent RSI when playing games. **(2 marks)**

1 Take regular breaks.

2 Use ergonomically designed equipment.

> Remember to make your answer relevant to the context – in this case gaming.

Now try this

target E-B

Describe **one positive** and **one negative** effect of ICT on an individual's health and safety. **(4 marks)**

The impact of networks

Networks connect us with the rest of society. This has an impact on the way we live.

Work
- **Teleworking** (working from home)
- Work easily with people **all over the world**
- **Location** of office less important
- Office/home networks allow users to share resources and have access to a range of resources
- Research for projects online

Communication
- Socialising with people all **around the world, 24/7**
- **Over use of** social networking sites
- Rapid spread of news

Networks

Creativity
- **Crowd sourcing** (people are collecting news and contributing content to websites)
- People become **content generators** for websites, for example YouTube, Wikipedia and Udraw

Shopping
- **Rapid** access
- **Round-the-clock** availability
- **No need to leave house**
- Research purchases more easily

Digital divide

Those who do not have access to networks are not able to access some information, goods and services. This is leading to a widening of the gap between the groups of people with and without access to networks, both within and between countries. For more information on the digital divide, see page 71.

Worked example

target
C-A

Describe **two** ways in which networks have an impact on society.   **(4 marks)**

Networks have a big impact on the way we work. They allow people to work from home but communicate easily with other people in offices and all over the world using email, VoIP and file sharing software. People can easily research ideas using the wealth of resources the Internet offers from all round the world. Networks also impact on how we buy things. We no longer need to leave our homes to go shopping and we can shop at any time of day, using the Internet.

Now try this

target
C-A

Explain how networks have changed the way information can be published.   **(3 marks)**

Remember: networks include the Internet, mobile phone network and home networks.

Legislation relating to the use of ICT

Laws passed by parliament are called **acts** or **legislation**. There are four acts you need to know about.

1   The **Data Protection Act (DPA)** protects us against misuse of our personal data that may be held by a range of organisations, for example shops, schools and businesses. These organisations must ensure that our personal data is:

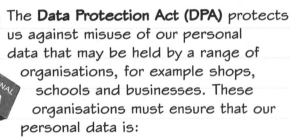

New laws need to be introduced continually to keep up with the developments in technology.

1. processed **fairly and lawfully**
2. obtained for **specified purposes**
3. adequate, relevant and **not excessive**
4. **accurate** and up to date
5. **not kept longer** than necessary
6. processed respecting the **rights of people**
7. kept **secure**
8. **not transferred** outside Europe.

2   The **Computer Misuse Act** covers the misuse of computer equipment and illegal access to files. This makes the following illegal and punishable by fines or imprisonment:

- software piracy (copying and distributing software illegally)
- planting viruses
- hacking
- fraud.

3   The **Copyright, Designs and Patents Act** makes it a **criminal offence** to copy or steal media or other people's work or ideas. For example, it is illegal to:

- **copy or distribute** media without a proper licence or the copyright owner's permission
- use purchased media on more computers than you have **licences** for.

4   The **Digital Economy Act** stops people illegally downloading media. Internet Service Providers (ISPs) can collect data about repeat offenders. If offenders continue downloading then their Internet access can be slowed or suspended.

Worked example

 target D-B

Sally buys a music CD from an online store.
Raj tells Sally that she can legally copy the CD because Sally has paid for it.
Explain why Raj is incorrect. **(2 marks)**

Sally's CD is for her own use. She cannot copy it without the copyright holder's permission. It is illegal to copy CDs in this way as stated in the Copyright, Designs and Patents Act.

EXAM ALERT!

In similar questions, students have shown a poor knowledge of legislation. It is important to understand how laws protect our rights.

Students have struggled with exam questions similar to this – **be prepared!**

ResultsPlus

Now try this

target B

Which **one** of these requires ISPs to take action against people who illegally download media?

(1 mark)

☐ **A** Data Protection Act   ☐ **C** Copyright, Designs and Patents Act
☐ **B** Computer Misuse Act   ☐ **D** Digital Economy Act

Unequal access to ICT

The **digital divide** is the gap between people who do not have access to digital technology and those who do. Because of the importance of digital technology in our modern lives, those who do not have access to ICT can be disadvantaged in many ways.

Causes of unequal access within the UK:

Affordability Those on low incomes may not have access to digital technology

Disability or illness can make it difficult for people to get access to ICT

Lack of knowledge and skills prevents people using ICT

People living in remote areas may not have access to Internet or mobile phone coverage

Cultural factors – gender inequalities and religious beliefs can restrict access

Causes of unequal access worldwide:

Affordability More wealthy countries have better access to digital technology

Limited access to electricity Countries without a reliable electrical supply have less access

Censorship Some governments restrict and censor access to digital technology

Implications of the digital divide

Economic
- People with good IT skills tend to get better paid jobs
- The Internet gives people access to a wider range of goods and services
- Access to the Internet allows people to research products and get cheaper deals
- The Internet has led to a rise in e-commerce and globalisation
- Countries without good access to ICT are developing more slowly

Educational
- Students who use computers tend to do better at school
- People with access to online courses can improve their skills and knowledge
- Students need technology to make the most of schools' personalised learning using VLEs

Social
- People with access to email, mobile phones and social networking can keep in touch more regularly with friends and family
- People can feel 'left out' if they do not have access to digital technology
- Children with access to technology may play on games consoles rather than playing outside

Cultural
- Some religious groups restrict their members' access to digital technology
- People may be stereotyped by gender: for example, boys and men may be given more access to, and education in, technology than girls and women

Worked example

 edexcel

target C

Michael uploads a podcast to his blog. Some people cannot access the podcast.
State **two** causes of unequal access to ICT.

(2 marks)

1 People cannot afford more recent technology.

2 They do not have the skills to be able to use it.

EXAM ALERT!

Less than a third of students gained both marks. Some did not give the causes which were asked for, but gave examples of the technology people without access to ICT would lack.

This was a real exam question that a lot of students struggled with – **be prepared!**   Results**Plus**

Now try this

target C

State **two** causes of the digital divide in the UK.   **(2 marks)**

Safe and responsible practice

Many people use digital technology in their homes. Users can keep safe by following these responsible practices.

Computer equipment emits **heat**.
- Keep the room well ventilated.

Digital devices can overheat and become a **fire hazard**.
- Fit smoke detectors and fire extinguishers.
- Do not overload electrical sockets.

Harmful bacteria can live on surfaces.
- Keep the computer and work surfaces clean.

Spilt drinks can cause an **electric shock** or damage your computer.
- Keep food and drink away from equipment.

Risks and responsible practice when using ICT

Incorrect use and positioning of equipment can cause **health problems**.
- Use ergonomically-designed equipment.
- Take breaks or change position regularly.

Use of computer equipment can cause **eye strain**.
- Keep the room well lit.
- Take regular screen breaks.

Another potential health and safety risk in the image is the overloaded plug socket.

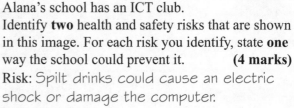

Worked example

target D-B

Alana's school has an ICT club.
Identify **two** health and safety risks that are shown in this image. For each risk you identify, state **one** way the school could prevent it.   **(4 marks)**

Risk: Spilt drinks could cause an electric shock or damage the computer.
Prevention: The school could ban drinks from ICT suite.

Risk: Students slouching at desk could cause back problems in later life.
Prevention: Students should be encouraged to maintain good posture.

Now try this

target F-D

Helena uses her laptop over extended periods of time.
Give **two** health and safety risks to Helena that could be caused by this extended use.   **(2 marks)**

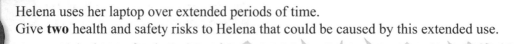

Sustainability issues

Sustainable development is development that meets the needs of the present without compromising the ability of future generations to meet their own needs.

Sustainability issues of ICT

E-waste
- Old computer equipment ends up as **electronic waste** (e-waste) that goes to landfill sites
- More developed countries are now sending e-waste to **less developed countries**

Pollution
- **Toxic substances** from e-waste can get into the soil and water supplies
- All digital devices **use electricity**. Large computers need even more electricity to keep them cool. The traditional generation of electricity produces greenhouse gases that can cause **global warming**

Finite resources
- Some of the elements used to create digital devices are in **short supply** so will run out one day
- Electricity often comes **from non-renewable** resources such as coal and oil (fossil fuels), which will also run out in the future

How to increase sustainability

Recycle
- **Recycle** or **reuse** old digital devices
- Donate unwanted digital devices to organisations who provide computers to poorer countries
- Companies will now buy your unwanted digital devices from you so they are **re-used**
- Some companies are now taking apart electronic waste and **selling the parts**

Reduce your impact
- Use digital devices for as **long as possible** before replacing
- **Switch off** digital devices when they are not in use and when batteries are charged
- Use devices that have a **sleep mode** when not in use

Renewable energy
- Companies who run large servers are now locating to locations with cool climates and **cheap sustainable electricity** (for example Iceland which has cool water for cooling and hydro electric power)
- Technology companies are starting to offer solar-powered devices

Worked example

target C-B

Debbie's computer is running slowly and she wants to replace it with a new one.

(a) Explain why Debbie should not just throw her old computer in the bin. **(2 marks)**

If she throws it in the dustbin, it will end up in landfill, which can result in toxic chemicals leaking into nearby soil and water.

target D-B

(b) Give **two** ways in which Debbie could dispose of it sustainably. **(2 marks)**

1 Debbie could recycle the parts.
2 She could donate it to a charity.

e-waste at a landfill site

Now try this

target E-C

Sally wants to buy a PC. She is worried about the amount of electricity it will use. State **two** ways in which Sally could minimise her use of electricity. **(2 marks)**

Scenario

At the beginning of each exam paper, you will find details of a **scenario**. This scenario gives you the **context** within which all exam questions are set. You should take a few minutes to read the scenario. It's important that you understand the scenario, and that you bear it in mind as you answer the questions on the exam paper. You will learn more about the scenario as you go through the exam paper because it follows the scenario throughout. The scenario is designed to:

- help you relate to the questions
- help you reuse ideas from earlier in the paper to answer later questions.

Worked example

target
F-E

Jack is going to buy a mobile phone for his <u>mother's</u> birthday. She has <u>never owned</u> a mobile phone before and has <u>poor eye sight</u>.

Give **two** <u>features</u> of a mobile phone that might make it more <u>accessible</u> to Jack's mother. **(2 marks)**

1 A key pad with large buttons.
2 A large, clear screen/display.

Savvy users will know lots of features of mobile phones. However, this question specifically asks you to give features that might make a phone **more accessible** to Jack's mother.

TOP TIP

It's a good idea to **underline** scenario details in the question that will help you when writing your answer, just as this student has done. Otherwise it's easy to give a general response that doesn't answer the question. If the student had given 'key pad' and 'screen' as their response, they wouldn't have received any marks.

Guided

target
D-C

David runs his own company making and selling car accessories. He has 20 employees in his factory designing and making the accessories. David bought desktop computers for his factory-based staff.

List **two** features of <u>desktop computers</u> that make them a good choice for staff <u>based in one location</u>. **(2 marks)**

Make sure you read the question carefully and underline the important words or phrases, in this case 'desktop computers' and 'based in one location'. You know lots of features of personal computers but don't just list the first two that come into your head. You need to sort through the features you know to identify those that are an advantage for people in a single location.

TOP TIP

Make sure that you apply what you know to the question asked. For example, one feature of desktop computers is that they need an electricity supply, however, this isn't what makes them a good choice for staff based in one location.

Command words

You need to pay attention to the **command words** used in exam questions. The command word gives you information about what **type of answer** you need to write. Here are some of the most common command words and what they tell you:

List	Your answer should be a list – the number of items you need to list depends on the number of marks available
State	
Identify	Your answer should be a simple sentence – the number of items you need to state/
Give	identify/give/name depends on the number of marks available
Name	
Describe	In your answer you should include details
Explain	In your answer you should make a point and then expand on each point (by giving examples or reasons) to make sure you are explaining the point
Discuss	You should compare different points of view, giving evidence to back up the points you make; you should reach a conclusion about the topic you have been discussing. Remember to think about spelling, punctuation and grammar

Worked example

The Smith family are trying to decide whether to install a cable or a Wi-Fi network in their home.
<u>State</u> what is meant by Wi-Fi.   **(1 mark)**

Wi-Fi is a method of transferring data wirelessly over a computer network.

target E

The command word in this question is 'state' so your answer needs to be a simple statement outlining what Wi-Fi is. Don't fall into the trap of writing down everything you know about Wi-Fi. All you need to do is to write down what Wi-Fi is, just as this student has done.

TOP TIP

It's a really good idea to underline the command word, just as this student has done.

Guided

List **two** benefits to the Smith family of installing a Wi-Fi network over a cable network.
          (2 marks)

target E-D

The command word in this question is 'list' so don't be afraid to write your answer as a numbered list. You don't need to go into the benefits in any great detail – you just need to say what they are.

TOP TIP

If you're writing your answer as a list, make sure you number your points so that your answer is clear.

Reading the question

It's really important that you **read the question**. This may sound simple, but lots of students lose marks because they haven't read the question properly.

> Stevie logs into a site to buy some music. She sees this symbol in her browser which tells her that data on the site is encrypted.
>
>
>
> State **one other** way that browsers display security information. **(1 mark)**

You need to pay attention to how many things you are asked to include in your answer:

- If asked for one way, just give one. Don't write down as many ways as you can think of.
- If asked for **two** ways, make sure you give **two**, and make sure they're **different from each other**.

A common mistake is to repeat the information given in the question. In a question similar to this, lots of students lost marks because the answer they gave was 'the padlock symbol'. The question mentions the padlock symbol and clearly asks students to give 'one other way'.

Worked example

target E-D

Ryan decides to buy flight tickets online. Before he pays, he signs up for an online account.

Give **two** advantages to Ryan of using an online account to buy flight tickets. **(2 marks)**

1 He will be able to review his account history and previous bookings.
2 Next time he buys flight tickets, it will be quicker because his personal details will be saved.

It's easy to misread questions when you're under pressure. For example, in questions like this which relate to a specific online shopping experience, students often reel off the generic advantages of shopping online, rather than relating the advantages to the specific online shopping experience mentioned in the question.

TOP TIP

Always read the whole question and make sure that your answer relates to the context given in the question.

Guided

target E

Give **one** disadvantage to Jasmine of her web browser remembering her password for a website. **(1 mark)**

Take your time – it's easy to misread 'disadvantage' as 'advantage' when you're stressed.

TOP TIP

If you've got time once you've finished answering all the questions, it's a great idea to check your answers to make sure they make sense when read **alongside the question**.

Explaining with examples and reasons

Command words such as 'Explain', 'Describe' and 'Discuss' are often worth more than one mark per point made. This makes it important to expand your answer by explaining with examples and reasons. Remember – use your EEERs! Many students forget to do this, so fail to answer the question fully.

When expanding 'describe' questions, it is good to give examples. When 'explaining', it is best to give reasons.

When tackling a question like this, think about the context carefully as you may need to give examples that are relevant to a particular situation.

Worked example

target D-B

Explain **one** advantage to Naomi of paying using a third party payment processor rather than her credit card. **(2 marks)**

Third party payment processors stand between the customers and the retailers so payments are not made directly. The buyer transfers money to the third party, who then pays the seller, so the buyer's banking details are not passed to the seller at all. This helps to prevent fraud.

This student has given the advantage that payments are not made directly to the seller. She has then **expanded** her answer by **explaining** how this happens and giving **a reason** why this is important.

TOP TIP

When questions ask for advantages or disadvantages, look carefully at who it is an advantage to (in this case Naomi) and if there is a 'rather than' part of the question (in this case her credit card). An answer relating to 'fast digital payment' would not be acceptable because it is also true of credit card payment.

Guided

Describe **one** way in which online shops prevent risks to users when paying online by credit card. **(2 marks)**

target D-B

First think about the risks of paying online using a credit card. These could be that someone might look over your shoulder to see you typing in your credit card details on the screen, or that they might intercept them whilst they are being sent.

Then think of the ways in which an online shop could help prevent this risk. The command word is 'Describe', so remember to expand your answer by giving examples as to how the precaution you have given can help prevent the risk.

Avoiding common mistakes

Students sometimes do less well than they could in the exam by making mistakes that can be easily avoided.

When revising:

- Revise each topic at least three times and make sure you know the key terms in each topic.
- Make sure you learn about policies and legislation. These are areas in which students often perform poorly.
- Use past papers to practise, but make sure that you don't try to regurgitate the same answers in your own exam paper without reading the question properly.

In the exam:

- Read each question carefully.
- Make sure your answer is relevant to the context described in the question.
- Make sure you answer the question rather than just explaining a term.
- Don't just say something is 'free', 'cheaper', 'faster' or 'easier' without saying how or why.
- If a question asks for two examples of something, make sure your answers are actually different and not just two ways of describing the same thing.
- Try to answer all the questions.
- Leave time to check your answers at the end of the exam. Remember to check your extended answers for spelling, punctuation and grammar.

Worked example

target E-C

Jo uses an ebook reader to read novels whilst travelling.
Give **two** benefits to Jo of carrying an ebook reader rather than traditional paperbacks. **(2 marks)**

1 It is lighter, so easier to carry on journeys.

2 She can download new books immediately if she has an Internet connection rather than having to visit a bookshop.

Remember, answers to do with portability of the ebook reader are really the same as saying that it is light. Make sure you give two **different** benefits, as this student has done.

TOP TIP

Read back over your answers quickly to make sure that you have given different answers, and that you haven't made the mistake of giving the same answer in slightly different ways.

Guided

target E

Henry's camera has GPS tagging as a feature.
State what GPS tagging does. **(1 mark)**

Students answering questions like this often give general explanations of what GPS is rather than answering the question. Think about what GPS tagging is and how it is a useful feature on a camera.

Extended questions

Every paper has two extended questions worth 6 marks each. These usually start with the command word 'Discuss'. These questions usually require you either to consider both sides of an argument or to support a given point of view.

Your quality of written communication is also assessed on these questions. This is indicated with an asterisk (*).

How to tackle these questions:

- Plan your answer.
- Put your points in order so you can present them in a logical and clear way.
- Consider how to link your points together.
- When asked to consider both sides of an argument present a balanced discussion by including both sides and giving examples.
- When asked to support an argument, you should present that view and explain your answer with examples and reasons. You should then show that other arguments exist, but finally reiterate why the points supporting the argument outweigh those against.
- Carefully check your spelling, punctuation and grammar as well as clarity of expression to gain the quality of written communication marks.

Guided

*Safe and responsible practice is extremely important when using ICT in the workplace. Make a reasoned argument to support this point of view.** (6 marks)*

target
C-A*

Plan

Health and safety risks of ICT – serious

- Fire hazard due to overheating/overloading – keep well ventilated, don't overload, fire extinguishers.
- Spilt drinks can cause electric shock or damage to computer – no drinks nearby.
- Harmful bacteria on keyboards cause stomach upsets – keep surfaces clean.
- Incorrect use of equipment leading to back problems/eye strain – correct positioning, ergonomic equipment.

Possible arguments against:

- Expense – but time lost through illness or even fire is expensive.
- Time – but if people off work through illness, more time wasted.
- Not real problem – people's health is paramount.

Reiterate – extremely important to take seriously.

Note how this student has planned his answer with examples of both risks and the ways to prevent these risks.

He has also shown that he is aware of the fact that there are other opinions, but strengthens his own argument by countering those objections and demonstrating that his own viewpoint is more valid. He then summarises the original point.

TOP TIP

Make sure you plan your answer by jotting down each point you want to make. This will help you to include everything, in logical order, in your answer.

Personal digital devices

David has a team of five sales people who travel around selling car accessories that he produces. He has decided to buy new laptops for his sales team from this shortlist:

	Laptop 1	Laptop 2	Laptop 3	Laptop 4
Processor	2.1 GHz	2.8 GHz	1.6 GHz	2.4 GHz
Memory	4 GB	8 GB	1 GB	4 GB
Hard drive	500 MB	1 TB	160 GB	2 TB
Optical drive	DVD RW	Blu-ray Read only	None	Blu-ray Read and write
USB ports	4	6	2	4
Wi-Fi	Yes	Yes	No	Yes
Weight	3 kg	3 kg	2 kg	1 kg
HDMI port	No	Yes	No	Yes
Battery life	5 hours	4 hours	3 hours	6 hours
Monitor	15 inch	17 inch	10 inch	15 inch

Guided

David has decided to buy Laptop 4 for his sales team.
List **two** advantages of Laptop 4 over the others that make it more suitable for a travelling sales person.   **(2 marks)**

 target E-D

You need to apply your knowledge when answering questions like this. In this case you need to identify features that are genuine advantages for someone who does a lot of travelling.

TOP TIP

Think about it carefully. Laptop 4 has a read and write Blu-ray drive whereas none of the other laptops do but is this really an advantage for someone who does a lot of travelling?

 Now try this

Jack, his wife and their daughter, Rosie, are going on holiday. Rosie wants to buy a digital camera to take with them. Jack wants to take all the holiday photos on his smartphone.

target D-C

(a) Give **two** reasons why a digital camera might take better photos than a smartphone.   **(2 marks)**

target B-A

(b) Rosie has found a digital camera that has GPS and the description states that it will allow geotagging of photos.
   (i) Explain how geotagging works.   **(2 marks)**

target D-C

   (ii) Jack warns Rosie not to upload geotagged photos to social networking sites.
   Explain why Rosie should not upload geotagged photos.   **(2 marks)**

Jack and his family are back from their holiday. Rosie is trying to persuade her dad to buy her a games console.

 **target C-B**

(c) Rosie thinks that games consoles are better than PCs for gaming.
   State **two** advantages of using consoles, rather than PCs, for gaming.   **(2 marks)**

target E-D

(d) Modern games consoles are multifunctional devices.
   Apart from gaming, give **two other** uses for games consoles.   **(2 marks)**

Connectivity

Guided

target D-C

Pay attention to the command word. In your answer, you need to make a point and then expand that point with an example or a reason.

Emily Jones is trying to persuade her parents to set up a home network.
Explain **one** benefit to the family of installing a network. **(2 marks)**

TOP TIP

Don't forget to take the context into account. You know lots of benefits of setting up a home network, but you must relate one of these benefits 'to the family' in your answer.

Now try this

target G

(a) State a peripheral that the Jones family will be able to share over the network. **(1 mark)**

target E

(b) Mr Jones has an old desktop computer. Suggest **one** piece of equipment he will have to install in it if he wants to connect to the network. **(1 mark)**

target C-A*

(c) Emily Jones likes to play computer games and wants her parents to install a cable network.
Explain **two** features of a cable network that would make Emily's online gaming experience better than if she uses a Wi-Fi network.

(4 marks)

target E

(d) Paul Jones is doing his GCSEs and he often uses the Internet to help him with his homework.
What is the name of the protocol (set of rules) the web browser uses when it is receiving data from a web page? **(1 mark)**

☐ **A** SMTP
☐ **B** HTTP
☐ **C** XML
☐ **D** HTML

target F-E

(e) Mrs Jones likes to make voice calls over the Internet using Voice over Internet Protocol (VoIP).
List **two** items of hardware she will need to connect to her computer to make these calls. **(2 marks)**

target G-F

(f) Mr Jones has bought a new laptop. He is a keen photographer and wants to upload his images to an online album. Suggest **two** methods he could use to transfer the images from his digital camera to his laptop. **(2 marks)**

For more information on the advantages and disadvantages of cable and Wi-Fi networks, see page 20.

Operating online

Guided

target **D**

Steve is asked for a memorable phrase when he is setting up an online account. This will be used in a challenge response test to control access to his online account.

Give **one other** example of the type of information that could be used in a challenge response test. **(1 mark)**

In questions like this, students often fail to gain the mark because they don't notice that they're being asked for 'one other example'. If you fail to see 'other' in the question, you might be tempted to give an example of a memorable phrase, such as mother's maiden name or first pet's name. Instead, you need to give one other type of information that can be used in a challenge response test.

TOP TIP

Make sure you read the question carefully. Some students find it helpful to underline the key words in the question.

Now try this

Catherine has decided to sign up for a broadband Internet account and is selecting an Internet Service Provider.

target **E–C**

(a) Give **three** features of an Internet Service Provider that Catherine should consider before buying a contract. **(3 marks)**

(b) Catherine uses the Internet to shop online. When she fills in forms to set up accounts, she often has to enter letters similar to those shown below:

Characters: [   ]
Enter the 8 characters you see

target **G**

(i) This is called a
☐ **A** Presence check
☐ **B** Validation check
☐ **C** Captcha test
☐ **D** Verification test **(1 mark)**

target **E–D**

(ii) Explain why these are used. **(2 marks)**

target **F**

(c) Catherine uses her credit card to pay for goods. State how she can check that the website is secure before she enters her card details. **(1 mark)**

(d) Catherine is concerned that the companies who store her personal details may misuse it.

target **D–C**

(i) State **two** requirements that the Data Protection Act (1998) places on people who store electronic data. **(2 marks)**

target **B–A**

(ii) State **two** rights that Catherine has under the Data Protection Act (1998). **(2 marks)**

target **C–A***

(e) *Like other people, Catherine is concerned about her security and privacy when she uses the Internet. Discuss how people and organisations can obtain Catherine's personal details and what she can do to minimise the risks. **(6 marks)**

Online goods and services

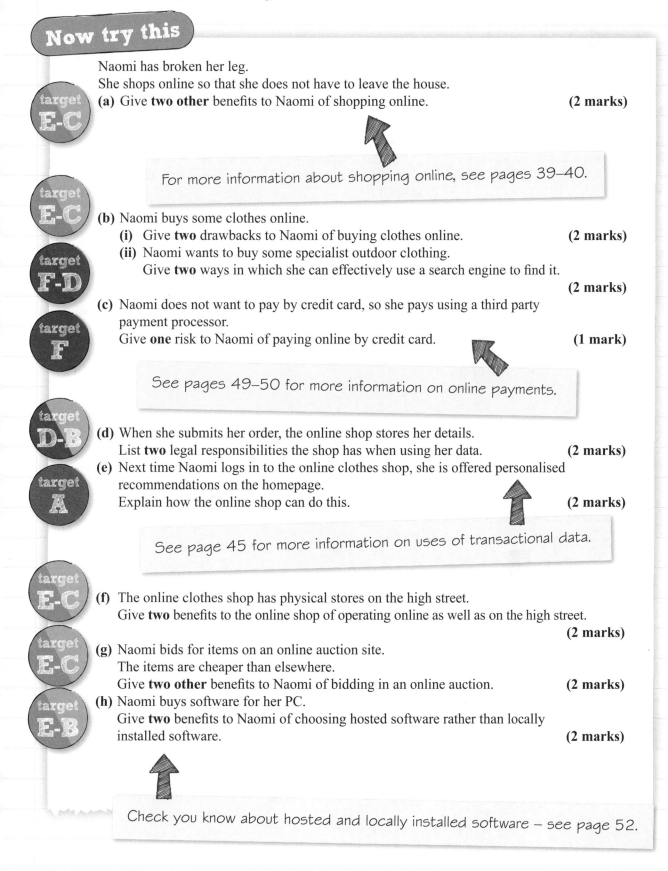

Now try this

Naomi has broken her leg.
She shops online so that she does not have to leave the house.

target E-C

(a) Give **two other** benefits to Naomi of shopping online. **(2 marks)**

For more information about shopping online, see pages 39–40.

target E-C

(b) Naomi buys some clothes online.

(i) Give **two** drawbacks to Naomi of buying clothes online. **(2 marks)**

target F-D

(ii) Naomi wants to buy some specialist outdoor clothing.
Give **two** ways in which she can effectively use a search engine to find it.
(2 marks)

target F

(c) Naomi does not want to pay by credit card, so she pays using a third party payment processor.
Give **one** risk to Naomi of paying online by credit card. **(1 mark)**

See pages 49–50 for more information on online payments.

target D-B

(d) When she submits her order, the online shop stores her details.
List **two** legal responsibilities the shop has when using her data. **(2 marks)**

target A

(e) Next time Naomi logs in to the online clothes shop, she is offered personalised recommendations on the homepage.
Explain how the online shop can do this. **(2 marks)**

See page 45 for more information on uses of transactional data.

target E-C

(f) The online clothes shop has physical stores on the high street.
Give **two** benefits to the online shop of operating online as well as on the high street.
(2 marks)

target E-C

(g) Naomi bids for items on an online auction site.
The items are cheaper than elsewhere.
Give **two other** benefits to Naomi of bidding in an online auction. **(2 marks)**

target E-B

(h) Naomi buys software for her PC.
Give **two** benefits to Naomi of choosing hosted software rather than locally installed software. **(2 marks)**

Check you know about hosted and locally installed software – see page 52.

Online communities

Now try this

Frankie is a member of two social networks. She uses one to communicate with friends and family. The other is a fashion network.

target B-A

(a) Explain why these social networks might have different features. **(2 marks)**

(b) Frankie has created a profile. Explain why she has done this. **(2 marks)**

target E-D

(c) Frankie meets Jade on the social network.
They become friends and Jade asks to meet in the real world.
Give **two** things Frankie could do to keep safe. **(2 marks)**

Since joining the social networks, Frankie often spends less time with her school friends face-to-face.

target D-C

(d) Give **two other** drawbacks to Frankie of using social networks. **(2 marks)**

target D-B

(e) Frankie never tells anyone else her password.
Give **two other** examples of acting responsibly when using of a social network. **(2 marks)**

See page 58 for more information on social networking.

Frankie's school uses a Virtual Learning Environment to store homework assignments.

target D-B

(f) Give **two other** functions of a Virtual Learning Environment. **(2 marks)**

target C-B

(g) Give **two** advantages to Frankie of using a Virtual Learning Environment. **(2 marks)**

target C-A*

(h) *Discuss the impact of the Internet on the way people work. **(6 marks)**

To revise Virtual Learning Environments, see page 57.

Frankie uses a variety of websites including wikis and social bookmarking sites.

target E

(i) Give **one** collaborative feature of a wiki. **(1 mark)**

target C-B

(j) Give **two** features of social bookmarking websites. **(2 marks)**

For more information on user-generated reference sites, see pages 59–60.

Issues

Now try this

A group of ICT students has been asked to give a whole school assembly on 'ICT issues'.

target C

target E-A

(a) Toby prepares a section on security issues.

(i) State what is meant by 'phishing'. **(1 mark)**

(ii) List **two other** security threats and state how each could be prevented. **(4 marks)**

target C-B

target B

(b) Erin knows that some people do not understand about cookies.

(i) Explain why online shops store cookies on customers' computers. **(2 marks)**

(ii) Give **one** reason why cookies might be considered a privacy issue. **(1 mark)**

You can find out more about cookies on page 66.

Nimesh is going to discuss how ICT can be used to monitor what we do.

target D-C

(c) It is possible to track friends' locations using their mobile phones. Give **one** potential **benefit** and **one** potential **drawback** to individuals of this functionality. **(2 marks)**

target B-A

(d) Government databases store details of digital communications. Explain **one** way in which this information might be useful to the government. **(2 marks)**

Make sure you know about how ICT can be used to track communication and movement. See page 67.

target C-B

(e) Shan is going to talk about health and safety when using ICT.

(i) Explain **one** way that ICT can benefit people's health and safety. **(2 marks)**

(ii) Give **two** health and safety risks associated with using mobile phones. **(2 marks)**

target C-B

target E

(f) Hiren is going to discuss issues to do with sharing digital media.

(i) Explain why illegal file sharing has a negative impact on digital artists. **(2 marks)**

(ii) Name **one** piece of legislation that covers the illegal copying of copyright material. **(1 mark)**

Health and safety is important when using ICT. For more information see page 68.

Need help on legislation? See page 70 to help you revise.

target D-C

target C-B

target F-B

(g) Ruby will be talking about the digital divide.

(i) Give **two** causes of unequal access to ICT. **(2 marks)**

(ii) Give **two** ways that a lack of access to the Internet may impact on school children. **(2 marks)**

(h) Rosie is going to talk about how to use devices safely. Give **three** examples of safe and responsible practice when using digital devices. **(3 marks)**

target B-A

target C-B

(i) Louis will be discussing sustainability of ICT.

(i) Explain what is meant by 'sustainability of ICT'. **(2 marks)**

(ii) Give **two** ways organisations can increase sustainability of ICT. **(2 marks)**

Glossary

3G
Third-generation wireless communication which allows high-speed wireless data transfer.

Acceptable use policy
Rules to which users agree, to reduce the misuse of ICT. Often found on social networking/collaborative sites.

Application (Applications software)
Software that helps users perform particular tasks.

Backup
A copy of data that is made in case the original data is lost or damaged. The backup can be used to restore the original data.

Bandwidth
The amount of data that can fit through an Internet connection. You can compare it to a ten-lane motorway which can fit more cars on it than a four-lane motorway. Bandwidth is measured in bits per second (bps). This indicates the number of bits of information that can fit down the line in one second. Kb or Kbps means thousands of bits per second; Mb or Mbps means millions of bits per second.

Biometric
An automated method of recognising a person based on physical characteristics. Among the features measured are face, fingerprints, hand geometry, iris and voice.

Blog
A shared online journal where people can post diary entries about their personal experiences and hobbies.

Blue-jacking
The sending of unwanted messages to others over Bluetooth connections.

Bluetooth
Allows the exchange of data over short distances from fixed and mobile devices. In order for devices to communicate they must be able to understand the Bluetooth rules (protocols).

Blu-Ray
A disk that enables the recording, rewriting and playback of high-definition video and the storing of large amounts of data. It has more than five times the storage capacity of traditional DVDs and can hold up to 25 GB on a single-layer disk and 50 GB on a dual-layer disk.

Broadband
A high-speed connection to the Internet.

Buffering
Downloading a certain amount of data into temporary storage before starting to play a file.

Card Code Verification (CCV)
A set of numbers on the back of a credit card that help verify that the use of the credit card is legitimate.

Cloud computing
A system in which all computer programs and data is stored on a central server owned by a company (e.g. Google) and accessed virtually.

Collaboratively
Working together with other people.

Commercial
Related to a business.

Compatible
The ability of a device to communicate and share information with another device.

Computer Misuse Act
This law restricts people from accessing or modifying data without permission.

Convergence
When one device is developed to carry out functions that were originally performed by several different devices.

Cookies
Small text files that are sent to your computer from certain websites. They track your behaviour and transactions.

Copyright
Gives the creator of an original work exclusive rights regarding that work for a certain period of time, including its publication, distribution and adaptation.

Copyright, Designs and Patents Act
This law protects people's original work from being used without their permission.

Credit card
A plastic card, issued by banks, building societies, retail stores and other businesses, which enables a person to buy goods and services without the need for cash. The holder agrees to pay back the money borrowed at a later date, sometimes with interest.

Data
Symbols, characters, images and numbers are all types of data. When data is processed and acquires meaning it becomes information. Computers process data to produce information.

Data Protection Act
This law regulates how personal information is used and protects against misuse of personal details.

Debit card
Similar to a credit card, but the money is taken directly from the cardholder's bank account.

Digital divide
Unequal access to ICT for individuals or groups, usually due to financial, geographic, health or cultural reasons.

Digital Economy Act
This law protects copyright holders from criminals who illegally distribute copyrighted material (piracy).

Digital Rights Management
Allows the copyright holder or the owner of the media control over the number of viewings, plays and copies, and even which devices the media can be played or viewed on. If you download a film from iTunes, you cannot burn it on to a DVD because of the DRM encoded in the film.

Dongle
A small piece of hardware that connects to a computer and has uses including data storage and picking up Bluetooth and 3G signals. A dongle may be portable like a USB pen.

Download
Transfer of a file, e.g. a video, from a central computer to your computer.

DVD
DVDs offer higher storage capacity than Compact Discs (CDs) while having the same dimensions. Blank recordable DVDs (DVD-R and DVD+R) can be recorded once using optical disc recording technologies and supported by optical disc drives and DVD recorders and then function as a DVD-ROM. Rewritable DVDs (DVD-RW, DVD+RW, and DVD-RAM) can be recorded and erased multiple times.

E-commerce
Buying and selling goods electronically, usually over the Internet.

Electronic waste (e-waste)
Rubbish comprising of digital materials e.g. old computers.

Encryption
For security, data is translated into a secret code according to a set of rules in a special 'key'. To convert the data back into plain text, the receiver must also have the key.

Ergonomics
The design of equipment to increase the efficiency of the way it is used by the human body, to promote the health of users.

Etiquette
A set of rules that people try to abide by out of respect for other people around them.

Firewall
A system designed to prevent unauthorised access to your computer when connected to a network such as the Internet.

Flash memory card
Used for fast and easily transferable information storage in digital devices such as mobile phones, media players and cameras. Flash memory is known as a solid state storage device, meaning there are no moving parts. Everything is electronic instead of mechanical and so it is ideal for mobile devices.

Fraud
Tricking someone for personal gain or to damage them.

Geotag
To attach the exact geographical coordinates of longitude and latitude to a digital image, giving the location of where it was taken.

Globalisation
The increasing integration of economies and societies around the world, particularly through international trade.

GPS (global positioning system)
A navigational system used in many devices which gives current location.

Hacker
Someone who gains unauthorised access to a computer in order to obtain data stored on it.

HDMI (high-definition multimedia interface)
Required for connecting devices to show high-definition video.

HDTV
High-definition TV.

High definition (HD)
The picture on a TV screen is made of lines of pixels. In a conventional TV there are 625 lines, which are refreshed 25 times per second. HD has either 720 or 1080 lines, so it produces a clearer sharper picture.

Hosted software
Hosted software, also known as Software as a Service (SaaS), is accessed via a web browser rather than being installed on the user's computer.

Identity theft
A crime that involves someone pretending to be another person in order to steal money or obtain other benefits.

Information overload
Having so much information that the user feels overwhelmed.

ISP (Internet service provider)
A company that provides Internet access to its customers.

IP (Internet Protocol) address
The personal address of your computer (just like your home address), so that servers know where to send the information you have requested.

Glossary

Lag
Slow computer functionality often caused by high latency or low performance hardware.

Latency
The time delay between the moment something is initiated and the moment it becomes detectable.

Locally installed software
Software which is installed on the user's computer.

Microblog
Short messages which may include short sentences, individual images or video links. An example is Twitter.

Multifunctional
Having the ability to do many different things using the same device.

Near field communication (NFC)
Allows the wireless exchange of data between two devices by touching them together or holding them very close to each other.

Non-physical goods
Items for sale which are delivered digitally e.g. music files from iTunes. Sometimes called DLC (downloadable content).

On-demand entertainment
Technology that allows users to view programmes at the time of their choosing by streaming them.

Online banking
A service offered by banks that allows account holders to view their account information online and carry out various financial transactions.

Online community
A group of members of a website who communicate and share ideas online, often about a shared interest.

Open source software
Software that is available to download free of charge, e.g. OpenOffice.org, which is a suite of applications.

Overheads
The ongoing expenses of operating a business, e.g. rent, fuel bills, salaries.

Peer-to-peer (P2P)
Sharing files among groups of people who are logged on to a file-sharing network.

Peripherals
External devices connected to a computer e.g. printer, microphone.

Personalised learning
Learning that is tailored towards the individual to allow them to make progress.

Personalisation techniques
Ways of making content relevant to a particular customer using their interests, geographical position, etc.

Phishing
A form of Internet fraud that aims to steal valuable information such as credit card details, usernames and passwords.

Physical goods
Items for sale which can be touched and must be delivered by post in some way.

Plagiarism
Copying someone else's work and presenting it as your own.

Privacy
The protection of personal data.

Proprietary software
Software for which you have to pay for a licence to use (e.g. Microsoft Office).

Protocol
A set of rules used by computers to communicate with each other across a network.

Public domain
Materials that are available for anyone to use for any purpose (not subject to the laws of copyright).

Query
To search, usually when talking about a database.

Repetitive Strain Injury (RSI)
Damage caused to the muscles, tendons, ligaments, nerves or joints, usually because of repeating the same action.

RSS feeds
A web feed format used for content which is frequently updated e.g. news, in a standard format so it can be added to a variety of websites.

Sat nav
A device, usually used in a car, that gives directions based on information received from a series of satellites.

SD and SDHC cards
Secure Digital (SD) cards are one type of flash memory card which store up to 2 GB of data. Secure Digital High Capacity (SDHC) cards are another type of flash memory card and they are ideal for video cameras because they can store up to 32 GB of data.

Search engine index
A list of websites which has been compiled by the search engine which drastically increases speed of searching. The search engine will search its index, which takes milliseconds, rather than millions of files, which could take hours.

Social bookmarking
A way of organising, storing and managing links to online resources, allowing users to search them easily.

Social networking site
An online community where people can communicate and share information.

Software as a service
See *Hosted software*.

Smartphone
A phone offering advanced features, e.g. the ability to send emails, surf the Internet.

Spyware
Software that can be installed on your computer without your knowledge, which collects information about your logins and passwords and sends details to another computer on the Internet.

SSL (Secure Sockets Layer)
A method of encrypting data to provide security for communications over networks such as the Internet. TLS (Transport Layer Security) is a later version of SSL.

Stream
Content is sent in compressed form over the Internet and displayed by the viewer in real time. When streaming video, a web user does not have to wait to download a file to play it. Instead, the media is sent in a continuous stream of data and is played as it arrives on a special player.

Sustainability
Meeting the needs of the present without compromising the needs of future generations.

Target audience
A description of the people your products are aimed at. It could include their age, the language they speak, their special needs, or any other characteristics relevant to the scenario you are given.

Targeted marketing
Identifying a specific target audience by identifying preferences or other personal details and then creating promotional or advertising campaigns to match their preferences.

Teleworking
Working from home but staying in touch with others with the help of technology.

Third party payment processor
A business that offers customers an alternative fast, safe method to pay for online goods and services.

Transactional data
Data which is gathered as part of a user's online activity. When buying something online, this could include information about the product bought but also personal details from the buyer such as address and payment details.

Trojan
A program that appears legitimate but which performs some harmful activity when it is run. It may be used to locate password information, or make the system more vulnerable to future entry, or simply destroy programs or data on the hard disk drive. A trojan is similar to a virus except that it does not replicate itself. It stays in the computer doing its damage or allowing somebody from a remote site to take control of the computer. Trojans often sneak in attached to a free game.

Upload
Transfer a file from your computer to a central computer, e.g. your ISP.

User-generated reference sites
User-generated reference sites allow users to generate content collaboratively on a website to which others can refer to inform their research.

Validity
Based on truth, or reason. It is important to judge whether information found online is valid because it could be biased or untruthful.

Viral marketing
A marketing strategy that encourages people to pass on a marketing message to their friends. It uses interesting and entertaining content that people will want to share. Viral marketing uses multimedia to make the message memorable.

Virtual learning environment
An online system for education with areas for homework, classes, teacher and pupil space etc.

Virus
A program designed to cause other programs on a computer to malfunction or stop working altogether.

VoIP (Voice over Internet Protocol)
This technology is used to make telephone calls via the Internet, usually at a cheaper cost.

Wi-Fi (Wireless Fidelity)
It is similar to Bluetooth in that it is used to exchange data wirelessly, but the signals can travel greater distances.

Wikis
A type of website that encourages collaboration by allowing users to add, edit and remove content.

Answers

Personal digital devices

1. Uses of digital devices

Any **two** from:

- Look up delays to flights or trains.
- Go on social networking sites and stay in touch with friends.
- Send emails or instant messages.
- Send text (SMS) and media (MMS) messages.
- Update or read blogs.
- Upload images to online albums.

2. Using digital devices

Suggestions of issues people should be aware of when travelling away from home with personal digital devices:

- portability – weight/size/robustness
- multifunctionality
- compatibility
- power adapters/chargers
- region restrictions
- mobile networks
- data/roaming charges
- connectivity
- battery life
- sociocultural impacts
- additional storage
- availability of the Internet
- security of the device/insurance
- personal security.

Remember that the quality of your argument is important too.

3. Common features

1 No moving parts and so not easily damaged.

2 Can be used to transfer data between devices.

4. Input and output devices

Any **two** from:

- headphones
- speakers
- microphone.

5. Connectivity

(a) Bluetooth and Wi-Fi.

(b) Wi-Fi enabled speakers have a greater range than Bluetooth which means that Wi-Fi speakers would be more versatile/could have more options for placing around the house.

6. Mobile phones 1

(a) Multimedia Messaging Service (MMS) and emails.

(b) Improved screen resolution means that the movies look better on the mobile phones. OR Large storage means that better quality movies can be stored in the phone memory.

7. Mobile phones 2

Any **two** from:

- set a PIN
- password protect
- lock SIM card
- encrypt data.

8. Personal computers 1

1 Relatively inexpensive.

2 Fits easily on a desk alongside text books.

9. Personal computers 2

One of:

- possible RSI
- eye strain
- finger stress/pressure on fingers.

10. Cameras and camcorders 1

A digital zoom only 'crops' and enlarges that part of the image in the viewfinder and does not actually zoom into the picture. Optical zoom works by changing the focal length of the lens so that light from distant objects can be brought to a focus on the sensor.

11. Cameras and camcorders 2

Users can use Wi-Fi to upload their photos or videos to online albums or social networking sites without having to download the files to a computer first.

12. Media players 1

JPEG

13. Media players 2

(a) Any **two** from:

- Does not use as much storage space.
- No need to wait for file to download before watching video/downloading takes longer/(streaming) saves time.
- Allows user to watch live/real time video.

(b) Any **two** from:

- Video is not available to watch offline / cannot keep (own) a local copy / Internet connection unavailable.
- Limited availability for some streamed video.
- User experience is dependent on connection quality / playback might be affected by buffering / video might lag / video might freeze.

14. Games consoles 1

(a) Any **two** from:

- The computer can be used for work and running other programs but a games console can only be used for playing games, watching movies and online surfing.
- Can play more multiplayer online games with a computer but with a games console can only play with users of the same console.
- Can use the computer screen but a games console has to be connected to a TV or monitor.

(b) Any **two** from:

- A computer is likely to be more expensive than a games console with the same speed and graphics capabilities.
- A computer needs to be set up and have software installed whereas a games console is ready to play straight out of the box.
- You need a flat surface for a computer whereas you can play on a games console anywhere.

15. Games consoles 2

Suggestions of points that would be made to support the view that playing video games is beneficial. Remember that the quality of your argument is important too.

Mental development – spatial awareness and attention span

- Playing video games can provide many benefits to a user's physical and mental well-being.
- Playing games can improve a person's spatial awareness and hand–eye coordination. These skills can then be applied in other situations.
- Keeping track of objects and characters in a game can also improve visual attention skills and increase attention span.

Learning skills and specific subjects

- Games can be an effective tool for learning because they can improve thinking, problem solving, reasoning and memory.
- Specialist games can be used in education for teaching and learning in subjects such as history and languages. These games can encourage the user to develop an interest in, and liking for, a particular subject and encourage them to go on to further study.

Social skills

- In some games a user has to understand the views of other characters and this can improve their social skills. These can be improved by playing multiplayer games where the user has to interact and communicate with other players around the world.

Physical activity

- Some games and consoles such as the Nintendo Wii and Xbox Kinect encourage players to move about, dance and take part in physical fitness regimes.

Staying safe

- Finally, playing video games in a home environment prevents people from getting into trouble outside.

16. Home entertainment systems

Connect to the wireless network pair the devices to allow data sharing and allow the images from the phone to be accessed by the TV.

17. Satellite navigation 1

(a) **One** of:

- The sat nav / GPS device cannot pick up a good enough signal from the satellites.
- Loss of signal.

(b) Distractions, stress, or lack of understanding of device may cause an accident / stress.

OR

Incorrect positioning of device may cause a blind spot / affect visibility.

18. Satellite navigation 2

Any **two** from:

- Can deal with unexpected incidents / provide alternative routes.
- Provides traffic updates.
- Plots speed.
- Shows current location / position / where you are.

- Shows estimated arrival time.
- Shows distance to destination.
- Easily updatable.
- Can map petrol stations/motorway services on your route.
- Easier for people driving alone: audio prompts.
- Do not have to stop to look at map.
- Can be voice activated.

19. Impact on organisations

Any **three** from:

- Finding out information – online research.
- Specialist software – for learning in subjects such as languages, history and so on.
- Use of digital devices such as interactive whiteboards, digital cameras, GPS and geocaching.
- Use of portable devices such as laptops, netbooks, tablets and smartphones to access learning resources.
- Educational apps for smartphones.
- Virtual learning environments (VLEs) to allow students to access learning resources, view lesson plans and hand in homework using portable digital devices wherever they are in the world.

Connectivity

20. Home networks

(a) Any **two** from:

- Cheaper – only cost of a router.
- No building work needed for routing cables through the house.
- Can access the network from anywhere in the house.
- Can carry device from room to room and stay connected.

(b) Router.

21. Network security

(a) Any **two** from:

- Use a form of encryption.
- Change default passwords on the router.
- MAC address filtering.
- Stop the router broadcasting its SSID.
- Reduce transmitter power.

(b) Wireless networks need to be secured otherwise other people can access your network and use your Internet connection or steal data.

22. Combining technologies

(a) Any **two** from:

- Bluetooth.
- Insert SD card from camera into netbook.
- USB cable.

(b) If he sets his phone as a portable Wi-Fi hotspot or tethers the devices using a USB cable/then the netbook can join this network and use the 3G network to access the Internet and upload images.

23. Bandwidth and latency

Bandwidth is the number of bits that can go through a network in one second. To stream HD video, Jed will need high bandwidth, otherwise the video will keep pausing to wait for more bits to arrive.

24. Wi-Fi and mobile broadband

Wi-Fi has a greater bandwidth than 3G and will be better for uploading photographs and using Internet telephone services such as Skype. Wi-Fi 'hotspots' are provided by many cafés and restaurants so she will be able to get a free Internet connection rather than having to pay for her 3G connection.

25. Peer-to-peer networks

1 It has a much higher bandwidth – 250 Mbps compared to 25 Mbps.

2 It has a greater range – 200 metres compared to 60 metres.

26. Communication protocols 1

The mail server downloads the emails to John's computer and deletes them from the server.

With IMAP John would read the emails on the server. They would not be deleted and he could access and read them from any computer.

27. Communication protocols 2

HTTP

28. Security risks in a network

(a) A firewall is used to stop (or allow) data transmission to stop malicious sites from accessing data on a computer.

(b) Encryption randomises/encodes the data/data needs to be decoded/uses a key so that unauthorised users cannot access the data/authorised users (with key) can read it.

29. Physical security risks

(a) Any **three** from:

- Security key pads.
- Burglar alarms.
- CCTV.
- Locks.

(b) You could use a fingerprint scanner that reads a person's fingerprint and checks whether or not there is a computer account or file in the system for that fingerprint.

Iris recognition or other biometric methods would be acceptable but the answer must be a **description**.

Operating online

30. The Internet

Any **three** from:

- Some could be more expensive than others for the bandwidth they are providing.
- This will affect the speed of downloading and uploading.
- Email addresses for communication and space for a personal website should be included.
- A firewall and antivirus and antispam software should be provided.
- Some ISPs impose a limit on how much can be downloaded and charge extra if you go over the limit.
- You should be able to block access to selected websites.
- You might not be able to have access at all times and the ISP might not answer help lines quickly when you need help.

31. Internet use 1

Any **two** from:

- Only have to post one message / message is distributed more quickly.
- Allows chat (real-time conversation).
- SMS requires payment for each person receiving message.
- Can send message without mobile phone signal / with Internet connection.
- Can add metadata (such as geodata).
- People can comment on / discuss the message.
- Can add multimedia to the message.

32. Internet use 2

(a) People can communicate using emails which they can send to one or many other users at the same time. The messages are sent and delivered far more quickly than normal mail. They can also attach documents and images to the emails which they cannot do in a voice call.

OR

Instant messaging allows people to communicate using text messages in real-time and the Voice over Internet Protocol allows both voice and video calls and is often free for the users.

OR

People can let others know what they are doing by posting on their blogs and social networking sites and they can upload photos to their online albums to display images of the places they have visited. This allows them to communicate far more quickly and with lots of people at the same time.

(b) More people can work from home by using the Internet to communicate and collaborate with others. This is a great help for people caring for families or who are disabled.

OR

For their work, people can communicate with colleagues using emails, instant messaging and VoIP. This allows them to make decisions far more quickly.

OR

They can have face-to-face meetings using video conferencing without having to travel long distances. This saves money on travel costs and accommodation.

OR

They can remotely log in to a company's network to access documents, work schedules and so on allowing them to work from home or when they are travelling.

OR

Data can be stored online so that all remote workers can access it without having to travel into the office.

OR

Groups of remote users can access online hosted applications so that they can all work together and collaborate on the same documents without all having to be in the same place at the same time. This will save time and money.

33. Security measures

(a) If a person has forgotten their password they can prove their identity by repeating the answer they have given to a security question. The answer could also be asked for, in addition to a password, to increase the level of security.

(b) (i) A captcha test displays some letters and numbers in a font which is difficult to read. The user then has to read the letters and enter them using the keyboard.

(ii) The test assumes that the letters and numbers cannot be read or interpreted by an automated computer program that could then complete the form. They are testing that a human and not a computer program is trying to complete the form.

34. Personal spaces

Any **three** from:

- An individual's personal information could be made available to all in the social network.

- GPS tools now provide a means of publishing an individual's location.

- Individuals may appear in media when they are not aware. (For example photos / videos on social media or Google's 'Street view' service.)

- Users need to be careful of what they look at online and be aware of bullying and people pretending to be someone else.

35. Information misuse

(a) One of:

- It saves you having to type your password in again when you revisit the site.

- Your view of the website is personalised.

- You can receive customised recommendations based on your shopping preferences.

(b) Any **two** from:

- To free up storage space on your computer.

- To stop unsolicited personalised adverts.

- To stop organisations getting hold of your personal information / browsing habits.

- To stop people finding out about your personal information / browsing habits on a shared computer.

36. Preventing misuse

(a) Any **two** from:

- Contact the sender to opt out / unsubscribe.

- Filter her emails / block sender / mark address as spam.

- Change her email address.

- Deactivate her email account.

(b) (i) To help Alice by suggesting music she might like and to make adverts more relevant to her.

(ii) The store has tracked her previous transactions. The store matched that data with other items for sale.

37. Legislation

Any **three** from:

- The customer has a right to know that the data is kept secure and must be used only for the purpose it was provided.

- They have the right to look at and check the data held.

- They can demand that incorrect information is amended.

- They can demand that the data is not used in any way that could cause harm or distress.

- They can demand that their data is not used for direct marketing.

38. Copyright

(a) 1 The creators of the music are losing the money they need to create and record the music.

2 It leads to unemployment because of loss of revenue.

(b) Because copying copyrighted material is illegal.

Online goods and services

39. Online shopping 1

Any **two** from:

- Customer reviews of the book available to inform choices.

- Books rated by other customers.

- Customers able to see example pages from the book without leaving the house.

- Available to customers 24/7/365.

- Tailored recommendations given to customers for additional purchases.

40. Online shopping 2

Any **two** from:

- Catherine cannot try the coat on so the coat may not fit her.
- The photo and description of the coat may not represent it accurately.
- Catherine will have to wait for the coat to be delivered.
- Catherine may have to return the coat.

41. Online auctions

Any **two** from:

- No need to have a physical shop to sell items.
- Can sell as many or few items as they wish.
- No need to develop a website of their own.
- Potential market is much larger than might be – auction websites are popular across the world.
- They can receive safe payment from a third party payment processor, without having to give away their bank details.
- They can receive positive ratings from bidders so that other people know they are trustworthy.

42. Online education, news and banking

Any **two** from:

- She can view all transactions including historical ones.
- She can print copies of previous transactions.
- She can receive promotions from the bank.
- She can access her bank details from any location with an Internet connection 24/7/365.

43. Online gaming and entertainment

(a) One of:

- She can store her status in the game and any credits that she has accumulated enabling her to leave the game and return later to the same status and credits.
- She can personalise her character, which can be saved for future games.
- She can link a payment service to allow her to make in-game purchases.

(b) Sarah's computer sends messages about her action to a central server that tracks the movements of all the players. The server then transmits these messages to all the other players' computers.

(c) One of:

- Her computer / graphics card specification is too low.
- Her bandwidth is too low / connection speed is too slow.
- Latency is too high / too many delays on the connection.

44. How and why organisations operate online

Any **two** from:

- Operating online will help PetzRUs to reach lots of new customers who aren't local to their high street shops.
- It won't cost PetzRUs too much to set up an online operation, but it's likely to increase their sales significantly.
- Some existing customers will like having the choice of whether to go to an actual shop or shop online, which means that PetzRUs customers are likely to be more satisfied with the service and more likely to come back.

45. Transactional data

Any **two** from:

- To understand the buying habits of customers.
- To check stock control.
- To see sales trends.
- For targeted advertising campaigns.
- To create personalised adverts OR for personalised marketing.

46. Internet advertising 1

(a) Any **two** from:

- It can be targeted at particular customers.
- Statistics can be gathered from people clicking on adverts.
- It is cheaper than traditional advertising, for example TV adverts.
- It reaches a wide range of customers.
- It reaches customers much faster than traditional advertising.
- Can use customers to spread the message (viral marketing).

(b) Any **two** from:

- There are so many Internet adverts that people sometimes just ignore them.
- Users can block adverts.

- If the Internet advert annoys the customer because it clutters up the screen or slows down the loading of the page, it may make them feel less likely to buy or it might affect brand loyalty.
- Online adverts can be limited in size and therefore can generally only contain short messages.
- Limits target market to those with an Internet connection.

47. Internet advertising 2

(a) Any **two** from:

- Cookies.
- Transactional data from previous purchases.
- Social networking sites.
- Microblogging sites.
- Personal information from online profiles.

(b) Benefit – **one** of:

- If the content 'goes viral' it 'spreads' very quickly.
- It is cheap as the organisation does not have to pay for adverts.
- Memorable content means that people remember the brand name.

Drawback – **one** of:

- People may not pass the advert on, so it may fail.
- It can be expensive to design and make effective viral adverts.

48. Internet advertising 3

Any **two** from:

- They could send personalised emails based on transactional data.
- They could personalise adverts using past browsing and searching on other websites.
- They could offer relevant alternative products and favourite categories based on purchase history.
- They could offer recommendations based on what you have viewed or purchased.

49. Payment systems 1

(a) Any **two** from:

- credit/debit cards
- third party payment processors
- online coupons and eVouchers.

(b) Any **two** from:

- The URL changes from http to https (s stands for secure).
- A padlock symbol is displayed.
- The colour of the address bar has changed to green.
- Use sites showing 'Norton Secured' which adds a further layer of authentication.

50. Payments systems 2

She can enter the unique reference number from the voucher. This should show the amount she has on her eVoucher and allow her to select how much of the eVoucher to use.

51. Consumer protection

There is a seven day 'cooling off period' for Internet purchases.

52. Applications software

Locally installed software has to be installed on the computer or file server, whereas hosted software is not installed – it runs on a web server over the Internet.

53. Commercial response to SaaS

One of:

- Make their products more appealing and better quality by including more facilities and functions.
- Provide technical support, help services and training materials.
- Use copyright to protect their products to stop similar 'free' products being offered as a 'software service'.

54. Storage: local or online?

Any **two** from:

- Seb can use free online data storage.
- Seb can easily share his digital photos with others.
- The photos are automatically backed up.
- Seb won't need (additional) local storage.

55. Search engines

One of:

- Add more key words to narrow down the search.
- Search by the type of object you are searching for e.g. image, a web page, news, maps, videos to narrow down the search.
- Use the advanced search facilities of the search engine to select options that are relevant to your search.

- Search by date/language/location as appropriate to focus the search results.
- Use more than one search engine. Different search engines give different results.
- Use Boolean terms such as AND and NOT to filter the results to make them more relevant.

Online communities

56. Online communities – what are they?

(a) Any **two** from:
- social networking
- online work spaces
- virtual learning environments
- wikis
- social bookmarking sites.

(b) Any **two** from:
- Your posts can be linked to you, so people can communicate with you more easily.
- Your preferences are saved.
- You can personalise your space.
- You can create an online social presence.
- Your account is secure so that only you can post under your name.
- People who use the community irresponsibly can be identified.

57. Online workspaces and VLEs

(a) Online workspaces provide a virtual space for people to meet/work together online collaboratively.

(b) One of:
- Easier to know which document is the most up to date (version control).
- Everyone involved in the newsletter can see edits to the documents as they happen.

58. Social networks

(a) Any **two** from:
- status updates
- friend requests
- chat
- messaging
- uploading video/images
- personal spaces for blogs and so on
- 'like' feature
- games.

(b) There are many social networks aimed at a specific target audience. They include features that the target audience would find useful. For example, LinkedIn is aimed at business people, so includes links to relevant vacancies and advice from industry experts.

59. User-generated references sites

Any **three** from:
- Able to add and edit the content.
- Changes can be tracked.
- Provides hyperlinked pages and images.
- Often uses moderators.

60. Social bookmarking sites

Users can tag URLs that can then be searched.
OR
URLs can be stored and then shared with other users.

61. Creation of knowledge

Any **two** from:
- Tools such as spreadsheets and databases within online workspaces help to create ideas, model different situations and solve problems.
- People can communicate, collaborate and share ideas on a global scale.
- Information is constantly updated and is always open for improvement, for example entries on Wikipedia.
- Users, rather than editors, can decide what information is important when they contribute to or rate Content online.
- Information and knowledge can be made accessible to everyone through ICT. University students can take courses and communicate with their tutors online.

62. Impact on working practices

Any **two** from:
- video conferencing
- VoIP
- email
- online chat
- social networking and online workspaces.

63. Socialising and responsible use

(a) Any **two** from:
- social networking
- blogging / microblogging
- online games
- chat rooms

- VoIP
- emails
- virtual worlds
- online dating.

(b) One of:

- Clare could block / defriend the user so that the user cannot send her more messages.
- Clare could report the user to the administrators so that they will monitor the other user and potentially withdraw his or her account.
- Clare could keep a copy of the material as evidence in case she needs to show it to the administrators / authorities later.

64. A global scale

(a) Any two from:

- social networking
- video conferencing
- VoIP
- cloud computing sharing data online
- blogs
- online workspaces
- user-generated reference sites
- social bookmarking.

(b) Use 3G on her mobile phone.

Issues

65. Security issues

Any **two** from:

- Set a PIN / password.
- Lock SIM card.
- Encrypt data.

66. Privacy issues

(a) 1 They save personal preferences so that you do not have to re-enter data.

2 They help websites to make more accurate suggestions about what you want to buy or view based on your browsing history.

(b) Any two from:

- Spyware – to intercept transactions.
- Hacking – to gain access to the computer.
- Copying personal information given on social networking sites.
- Sending phishing emails to obtain usernames and passwords.

67. Monitoring movements and communications

(a) Any two from:

- mobile phone location
- loyalty cards – where we shop
- credit / debit cards – where we use ATM machines
- passports
- GPS tracking.

(b) Any two from:

- SMS message
- emails
- social networking
- microblogging messages
- playing online games
- taking part in virtual worlds.

68. Health and safety

Positives – **one** of:

- Exercises at home using games such as the Wii can improve physical fitness.
- Health and fitness monitoring is made more accurate.
- Mobile phones can help us keep safe by always being able to contact others.
- GPS technology can help us to find our location and guide us along routes.

Negatives – **one** of:

- ICT can contribute to obesity due to inactivity.
- People can always access their work, even on holiday or in the evening, so can become ill or stressed as they feel they are unable to stop working.
- Repetitive strain injuries can develop from doing the same thing again and again.
- Joint pain can result from sitting incorrectly for a long time.
- Eye strain can be caused by staring at a screen for a long time.
- Accidents can be caused by people using mobile phones whilst driving.
- Hand-held GPS devices have resulted in accidents for mountain walkers.

69. The impact of networks

Networks connect us with the rest of society. That means that individuals can publish their own work directly onto the Internet in the form of their own blog or onto a wiki, for example Wikipedia. Books are also published digitally for download onto digital devices, and newspapers and magazines often have web versions which may be free or subscription based. Digital versions of books and newspapers and so on are increasing in popularity, whilst the printed equivalents are declining. This is because digital versions are more portable, regularly updated and sometimes free.

70. Legislation relating to the use of ICT

D Digital Economy Act

71. Unequal access to ICT

Any **two** from:

* affordability
* lack of knowledge and skills
* disability
* living in remote areas
* cultural factors – religion, gender, politics, censorship.

72. Safe and responsible practice

* Bad posture / RSI through incorrect positioning of equipment.
* Eye strain through staring at a screen for long periods of time.

73. Sustainability issues

Any **two** from:

* She could choose a device with a sleep mode when it is not in use.
* She could switch it off when not in use.
* She could buy an energy efficient device.

Exam skills

74. Scenario

Any **two** from:

* Desktops tend to have powerful processors and lots of RAM making it easier to switch between lots of applications.
* Desktops are easy to upgrade and enhance.
* Desktops tend to be more comfortable to use for extended periods of time, if set up properly.
* Desktops tend to last longer than laptops.

75. Command words

Any **two** from:

* It would be cheaper for the Smith family as they only need a wireless router.
* Can access the network from anywhere in the house (if within range).
* Can move from room to room without disconnecting from the network.

76. Reading the question

Could be a security risk because it allows other users of her computer to access her account without needing to know the password.

77. Explaining with examples and reasons

One of:

* Data encryption which puts data into a secret code that only people with the key can read. In this example, someone paying by credit card would enter their details, which would be encrypted by the website and would only be readable to the online shop.
* Asterisk characters could be used to prevent people seeing the numbers on screen, for example if someone were standing behind you as you enter your card number.

78. Avoiding common mistakes

One of:

* Shows where the image was taken.
* Adds coordinates to the images.

Question practice

80. Personal digital devices

Guided answer

1 It is the lightest laptop (only 1 kg) which makes it easier to carry.
2 It has the longest battery life (6 hours) which is useful to someone on the move who may not have access to an electricity supply.

Now try this

(a) Any **two** from:

* A digital camera will have a better lens.
* A digital camera will have optical zoom.
* A digital camera will have more features to let you enhance the image.

(b) (i) The exact coordinates of longitude and latitude are added to the file attached to the image giving details about it.

OR

The exact coordinates of longitude and latitude are added to the metadata.

(ii) If Rosie uploads geotagged photos people will be able to find out her location/where she is at a particular time which puts her in danger from stalkers.

(c) Any **two** from:

- Need to know how to set up PC/consoles are easier to set up.
- Consoles include ready-made controllers.
- Can play on consoles anywhere – don't need a desk.
- Consoles are compact/all in one/don't need extra peripherals for gaming.
- Consoles are designed specifically for gaming.
- Can play hands free/new gaming technology/games always on console first.

(d) Any **two** from:

- Accessing the Internet.
- Playing CDs, DVDs, Blu-rays/watching videos/listening to music.
- Social networking.
- Streaming/downloading video/music.

81. Connectivity

Guided answer

Having a home network will allow the family to share files, such as photos or music files, and it will also let them back up their important files on a different computer.

OR

Having a home network will allow all the members of the family to use the Internet simultaneously, without having to have multiple accounts with their ISP.

OR

Having a home network will allow the family to share peripherals, such as CD-burners and scanners.

OR

Having a home network will allow the family to play multiplayer computer games against each other by networking their computers.

Now try this

(a) Printer/scanner/webcam/CD-burner.

(b) Network Interface Card (NIC).

(c) 1 Higher bandwidth – more data per second can be transmitted meaning online games will operate at the correct speed.

2 Lower latency – there will be less of a time lapse between Emily clicking mouse/pressing a key and action occurring at the remote computer where the game is running.

(d) B HTTP

(e) Microphone/speakers or headphones.

(f) Any **two** from:

- Bluetooth.
- Cable, e.g. USB cable.
- Transfer flash memory card from camera to laptop.
- Wi-Fi.

82. Operating online

Guided answer

One of:

- PIN code/passcode/user ID.
- Choose a memorable image.
- Choose a memorable sound.
- Biometric (fingerprint, etc.)
- Captcha test.

Now try this

(a) Any **three** from:

- cost
- bandwidth
- download limits
- email and web space
- security
- parental controls
- reliability and support

(b) (i) C Captcha test

(ii) They are used to prevent automated software from filling in the form as this could lead to the production of email spam.

(c) The URL or web address will start with https.

OR

The padlock icon will appear in the address bar.

OR

You can double-click on the padlock to read the security certificate and check it is up to date.

(d) (i) Any **two** from:

- People who keep the data must process it according to the law.
- The data must be used only for the purpose for which it was provided.
- Firms should not ask for more data than is necessary.
- Firms should ensure that the data is accurate and kept up to date.
- The data should not be kept longer than is necessary.
- The firms should respect the legal rights of the people whose data they are processing (data subjects).

- The data should be kept secure.
- The data should not be transferred to other users outside Europe unless that country has similar laws to safeguard data.

(ii) Any **two** from:

- She can ask to look at and check the data held (but companies can charge for this).
- She can demand that incorrect information is amended.
- She can demand that the data is not used in any way that could harm or distress her.
- She can demand that her data is not used for direct marketing.

(e) The following points would be valid in an answer to this question. Remember that the quality of your argument is important too.

How details can be collected – each to be explained:

Overt:

- Filling out online forms when creating accounts.
- Boxes to click about sharing information.
- Checking of privacy policies, profile, posts on blogs and social network sites.

Covert:

- Cookies.
- Spyware – Trojans.
- Phishing.
- Online sites checking transactions.
- Search engines keeping a record of users' searches.
- ISPs keeping records of online activity.
- Collection of GPS data.

Details given by other people:

- Other people can post pictures and details about you on blogs, websites and social networking sites.

An explanation of how to prevent Trojans:

- Never run programs unless they are from a trusted source.
- Never open email attachments unless the source is known.
- Update antivirus and security software regularly.
- Install patches and security updates when they become available.
- Always virus check CDs.

- Never accept programs transferred from instant messaging sites.

An explanation of how to recognise phishing emails:

- Impersonal salutation – does not include your name.
- Careless use of language and spelling and grammar mistakes.
- Have attachments which you are asked to download. They usually contain spyware.
- They have false links for you to click on.
- Have a sense of urgency which makes you react and reply without thinking.

Very good answers will include a balanced discussion showing knowledge and understanding of threats and how to prevent them. Spelling, punctuation and grammar will be used accurately.

83. Online goods and services

(a) Any **two** from:

- Far greater choice as you are not limited to one geographical area.
- You can shop all day, every day.
- You can find the best price using price comparison websites.
- You can read other users' reviews of a product.

(b) (i) Any **two** from:

- You need Internet access and computer skills.
- You cannot pay using cash.
- You can't see or touch products or try on clothes.
- You usually have to pay for delivery.
- You need to submit personal information through a website.
- There is a risk of not receiving goods or having personal details stolen on fraudulent websites.

(ii) Any **two** from:

- Be careful with choice of key words.
- Add more key words to narrow down the search.
- Search by the type of object, for example image, a webpage, news, maps, videos.
- Use the advanced search facilities of the search engine.

- Use more than one search engine. Different search engines give different results.
- Use Boolean operators (AND, OR, etc.) to gain more specific results.

(c) One of:

- The details can be 'seen' as they are sent over the Internet.
- The data could be viewed on screen by someone standing near the user.
- A criminal who had stolen personal details could steal their identity and order using their details.

(d) Any **two** from:

- To keep it secure.
- Not to ask for more data than necessary.
- Not to keep data any longer than necessary.
- To keep data accurate and up to date.
- Not to use data for any other purpose without her consent.
- To process data fairly and lawfully.
- To process data respecting the rights of people.
- Not to transfer the data outside Europe.

(e) The store has tracked data from her previous transactions in her account or through cookies and has stored that information in a database. They have queried the database and sent her an email about similar products.

(f) Any **two** from:

- Online businesses can be located anywhere, so don't have to pay expensive high street rental prices.
- They also often need less staff, which saves money.
- Because online businesses don't physically display their stock they can usually carry a greater range of products.
- They can also attract customers from all over the world.

(g) Any **two** from:

- The ability to search easily for items that you want.
- A community of users which builds trust by rating both buyers and sellers.
- Third party payment options for secure payments.

(h) Any **two** from:

- Doesn't take up any file space on your computer.
- Hosted software is backed up by the server.
- Naomi doesn't have to update the software as updates are done on the host server.
- Naomi can use the software on any computer with Internet access.

84. Online communities

(a) The features of the fashion social website will be tailored to the target audience, so will offer features that will interest them. For example, it may have the feature to post reviews of clothes that have been bought to inform others thinking of buying the same thing, or to ask questions direct to a fashion house or manufacturer.

(b) Frankie's profile enables her to build an online presence including details about herself and her interests, so people who are interested in the same things can befriend her and talk to her. Her profile also enables her to submit content.

(c) Any **two** from:

- Take a trusted adult.
- Meet in a public place.
- Meet in the daytime.
- Let her parents know when and where she is going.
- Ask Jade to meet up on a webcam first.

(d) Any **two** from:

- Some people create fake profiles, so you don't really know who to trust.
- Loss of privacy if too much information is offered.
- You need to keep up to date with the privacy settings to protect your content.
- Online bullying.
- Posting content such as compromising photos may prove embarrassing.

(e) Any **two** from:

- Respecting other people's computers and files.
- Keeping your computer as safe as possible by using antivirus software and firewalls.
- Respecting other people's opinions online.
- Thanking and acknowledging people online.
- Honouring the copyright laws by not making unauthorised copies of files.
- Not posting inappropriate images or videos.

(f) Any **two** from:

- Provide information to help students learn, for example access to additional notes and homework, in school or remotely from home as long as they have an Internet connection.
- Allow teachers to work collaboratively to create high quality learning material.
- Allow personalised learning for individual students.

(g) Any **two** from:

- Timetable/'news' for staff and students.
- Students upload assignments for marking.
- Students can receive marks and feedback.
- Email and chat communication.
- Students can track progress and data such as test marks.
- Subject-specific links and learning resources.
- Personalisation for individual students.
- Interactive polls and questionnaires.
- Facility for students to contribute to blogs and personalise their own space.

(h) The following points would be valid in an answer to this question. Remember that the quality of your argument is important too.

Advantages

- Efficient collaboration/sharing through online workspaces/cloud computing.
- Problems can be solved more efficiently through video conferencing, VoIP, email, online chat, social networking.
- Saves money and reduces pollution as people can telework.
- People can work on a global scale much more efficiently.
- Employers can check social networks to research potential employees.

Disadvantages

- Less social contact.
- Easy to work for long hours with no break/distractions at home.
- Effective workers without access may be left out of making important decisions.
- Some employees have been disciplined for making defamatory posts on social network.
- Workers can be distracted from their tasks by websites (e.g. social networks).

(i) Content can be edited by multiple users.

(j) Any **two** from:

- Can store URLs online.
- Users give tag words to categorise the URLs.
- The tags can then be used to search bookmarks by topic/category.
- You can share your bookmarks with others online.
- You can search for similar bookmarks from other users using tags.
- Users can like or dislike content.

85. Issues

(a) (i) Phishing 'cons' people into believing that an email or text is from a valid organisation so that they give away their username and passwords leading to identity theft.

(ii) Any **two** security threats from:

- Physical threats, for example fire, flood.
- Hackers accessing your data.
- Unsecured wireless networks allowing others to see and use your network.
- Cookies which make it easier for others to gain access to your accounts.
- Viruses which harm your computer.
- Bluejacking – where unwanted messages can be sent to open Bluetooth connections, for example to people's mobile phones.

Any **two** methods of prevention from:

- Keep computers in locked rooms and back up the data.
- Use firewalls, passwords and encrypt the information travelling across networks.
- Secure wireless networks using a password and encrypt data travelling over the network.
- Know how to delete and manage cookies by using options in the browser.
- Use up-to-date antivirus software and take care when downloading files.
- Keep Bluetooth switched off when not in use.

(b) (i) Any **two** from:

- Target online ads.
- Provide recommendations for similar products based on browsing/purchasing history.
- Keep items in the shopping basket – convenient for the customer.

- Store customer information so that the customer does not have to type in the same information multiple times.

(ii) Cookies may be seen as a privacy issue as other people may be able to gain access to them and find out the personal information that is stored within them.

(c) Benefit – **one** of:

- They can locate friends so know if they are running late, or where they are so you can meet them.
- If a friend goes missing with their phone, they can be located.
- Police can track known criminals, making the world safer.
- If someone mislays their phone, they can locate it using friends' technology.

Drawback – **one** of:

- Friends will be able to track you at any time as long as your mobile is on.
- Other people may be able to track you and know places you regularly visit if your friend's phone gets into someone else's hands.
- Although you need to give permission for friends to track you, if someone has five minutes access to your phone, they can give that permission without your knowledge.

(d) If the government suspects that a person is a criminal, for example a terrorist, they can track their communications and gain proof so that they can arrest them and prevent a serious crime.

(e) (i) Exercises at home using games such as the Wii can improve physical fitness.

(ii) 1 RSI

2 Accidents on the road can be caused by people using mobile phones.

(f) (i) It costs time and money to produce digital media. Artists receive payment and acknowledgement for their work. Copying digital media means artists do not receive this payment and this may result in them not being able to afford to produce any more.

(ii) **One** of:

- The Copyright Designs and Patents Act.
- The Digital Economy Act.

(g) (i) Any **two** from:

- Affordability – those on low incomes or who are unemployed may not have access to digital technology.

- Lack of knowledge and skills.
- Disability can make it difficult for people to get access to ICT.
- People living in remote areas may not have access to the networks they need to get Internet or mobile phone coverage.

(ii) Any **two** from:

- Students who use computers tend to do better at school.
- Students with access to online courses can improve their skills and knowledge, no matter where they live.
- Students need technology to make the most of schools' personalised learning using VLEs.
- Students can feel 'left out' if they do not have access to digital technology.

(h) Any **three** from:

- Keep the room well ventilated to keep the room at a safe temperature for people to work in.
- Rooms with computer equipment should have smoke detectors and fire extinguishers.
- Electrical sockets must not be overloaded.
- Food and drink should be kept away so it cannot be spilt on the computer causing an electric shock.
- Keep the computer and work surfaces clean to prevent bacteria.
- All the equipment including the keyboards and chairs should be ergonomic.
- Take breaks or change position regularly to prevent back problems and RSI.
- People need to be trained to use the digital devices effectively.
- The room needs to be well lit to prevent eyestrain.

(i) (i) Sustainability is about being able to meet the needs of the present without compromising the needs of future generations. For ICT, this means making sure that we can take advantage of the latest technology without polluting the environment for future generations.

(ii) Any **two** from:

- Recycle or reuse the digital devices.
- Donate unwanted digital devices to organisations who provide computers to poorer countries.
- Some companies are now taking apart electronic waste and selling the parts.

- Use digital devices for as long as possible before replacing.
- Switch off digital devices when they are not in use and when batteries are charged.
- Use devices that have a sleep mode when not in use.
- Companies who run large servers are now locating to locations with cheap sustainable electricity (for example Iceland which has cool water for cooling and hydroelectric power).
- Technology companies are starting to offer solar-powered devices.

Your own notes

Your own notes

Your own notes

Your own notes

Published by Pearson Education Limited, Edinburgh Gate, Harlow, Essex, CM20 2JE.

www.pearsonschoolsandfecolleges.co.uk

Copies of official specifications for all Edexcel qualifications may be found on the Edexcel website: www.edexcel.com

Text and original illustrations © Pearson Education Limited 2012
Edited and produced by Wearset, Boldon, Tyne and Wear
Illustrated and typeset by HL Studios, Witney, Oxfordshire
Cover illustration by Miriam Sturdee

The rights of Nicola Hughes and David Waller to be identified as authors of this work have been asserted by them in accordance with the Copyright, Designs and Patents Act 1988.

First published 2012

16 15 14 13 12
10 9 8 7 6 5 4 3 2

British Library Cataloguing in Publication Data
A catalogue record for this book is available from the British Library

ISBN 978 1 446 90387 2

Printed in Slovakia by Neografia

Acknowledgements
The authors and publisher would like to thank the following individuals and organisations for permission to reproduce photographs:

Alamy Images: incamerastock 50; **Digital Vision:** 58; **Shutterstock.com:** Blend Images 51, Huguette Roe 73

All other images © Pearson Education

The authors and publisher would like to thank the following individuals and organisations for permission to reproduce copyright material:

Google, Inc. for a screenshot on page 46 from the Google search 'Christmas Cards" and the Google logo on page 55, copyright © Google, Inc.; Yahoo! Europe Ltd for the Yahoo! logo on page 55, copyright © Yahoo!; Wikimedia Foundation Inc. for the Wikipedia logo on page 59, copyright © Wikimedia Foundation Inc.; and AVOS Systems, Inc. for the Delicious logo on page 60, copyright © AVOS Systems, Inc.

Every effort has been made to contact copyright holders of material reproduced in this book. Any omissions will be rectified in subsequent printings if notice is given to the publishers.

In the writing of this book, no Edexcel examiners authored sections relevant to examination papers for which they have responsibility.